women in family business

WHAT KEEPS YOU UP AT NIGHT?

D1280119

*For my mother—*PATRICIA ANNINO

*For Carol, my wife of 32 years, the best thing that ever happened to me.
I do not know where I would be without her.* —THOMAS DAVIDOW

*For my mother, Lois, who always let me know that I could achieve
any dream that I could conceive; that anything is possible. I will
always be grateful to her for that, and more importantly, for knowing
that I am always loved...there is no greater gift for a daughter than
that. I love you, Mom!* —CYNTHIA ADAMS HARRISON

Table of Contents

introduction

Family owned businesses in America continue to thrive today. With their creativity, continuity and contribution to their communities, they have made themselves an essential aspect of the U.S. economy, now and in the future.

The good news for women in family owned businesses is that their roles continue to grow in importance. Today's wife, mother, widow, second wife, daughter, daughter-in-law, sister and sister-in-law can expect to play a key part in the succession and continuity of the family owned business. But there is a caveat for women as well: While the number of women involved with the family business in this country is staggering, the resources tailored to them are scarce.

Women in Family Business: What Keeps You Up at Night? addresses the psychological, relational and practical issues associated with management and succession which impact the lives, in the short and long term, of today's and tomorrow's women in family owned businesses.

Women have always played important roles in family owned businesses—from keeping the home intact (allowing their spouses to devote the time necessary to build businesses) to Chief (formal or informal) Business Advisors, to co-founders, to CEO/Presidents.

As women's roles continue to evolve, they also bring with them specific challenges and concerns: Wives worry when their husbands, unable to face change or their mortality, won't step down and let their children run the business. Mothers worry that their children aren't being treated fairly or that appointing one of them as successor will disrupt sibling harmony. Widows aren't sure whether to keep the business or sell it. Stepmothers feel like outsiders in their blended families, with very limited influence over their stepchildren and too little financial security. Daughters and sisters want their fathers' approval and to be given as much responsibility and as many opportunities in the business as their brothers, without sacrificing the flexibility to raise a family. And daughters-in-law and sisters-in-law want their in-laws to treat them with respect, not like second class citizens.

As a team of advisors, each of whom has more than two decades of experience working with family businesses, we offer in this book our insights and solutions to all of these concerns. Through a combination of theoretical underpinnings; relevant anecdotes, highlighting the challenges women face in their family businesses; and concrete advice, we hope to heighten women's awareness of the psychological, relational and financial implications of their roles and to present them with a survival guide for taking care of themselves and their families.

PART I

wife

A successful marriage in the family business functions as a true partnership in which husband and wife manage everything that affects their relationship and family. When a wife understands that her family's quality of life is defined by the success or the failure of the family business, her role can be an enormous boon to her husband's success.

chapter one

BE INFORMED—BE INFLUENTIAL

My husband doesn't discuss the business with me. How do I find out what is going on?

It's both healthy and reasonable for you to want information about what is going on with the business. Here are three reasons why:

1. If your children are going to be entering into the family business, or already have, it's important that you and your husband discuss how they are performing and how to treat them fairly and reasonably.

2. Your family business may well be your most valuable asset. If you plan to pass it on to the next generation, knowing about its condition will help you assess the wisdom and possibility of doing so. If, for example, you have a child in the business who is not performing up, and one of you wants to continue to give him or her opportunities, the other one can explain in concrete terms the risk of doing that to your financial health.

3. For the sake of your own financial security, it's important for you to know the answers to the following questions as they pertain to the various stages of your life: What is my right to involvement in what you had before you married me? What's going to be transpiring as we go along? What is going on with the business? How are we going to retire? What happens if you become disabled? What are you doing with our wealth? How are you dividing it up amongst the kids?

The answers to these questions will clarify your financial future as well as any implicit, unstated contracts of your marriage.

GETTING YOUR HUSBAND TO TALK TO YOU

Suppose, in an attempt to find out about the business, you ask your husband how his day went and he doesn't want to talk about it. What do you do?

Your husband probably has his reasons. Perhaps he made a simple decision that day—he had to fire an employee or he had to buy a truck. His decision was most likely a consequence of so many events in his work environment, all of which you know little or nothing about because you are not there, that it may be too difficult for him to describe them or for you to follow. Or perhaps he is so tired after dealing with problems all day long that he doesn't feel like talking about it. Regardless of gender, when someone's inside an experience, it's hard to explain a decision and its context to someone who is outside of it.

How do you get past his reluctance and his exhaustion? Try saying to him, "You look tired. You look awful. You must have had an incredible day." By letting him know that you care, you open the door to communication. You may wind up hearing more than you need or want to know, but you can filter through it by asking questions.

If he still won't respond, *don't take it personally.* When you feel that he is rejecting you, or that you are the brunt of his frustration or weariness, remind yourself that his behavior has much more to do with him than with you.

MEN AND WOMEN REALLY *ARE* DIFFERENT

Men's self esteem depends upon their ability to stand apart. They need to appear to the world like they are in control of situations, even if they aren't. Not wanting to show their confusion or vulnerability to the outside world, they distance themselves from others, stand independently and shut down.

The distance they create scares women, whose self esteem rests on their ability to stay connected to others. A wife knows that she is doing her job and is good at it when her husband talks to her and is vulnerable with her. The opposing self-esteem dynamics—he shuts down because he needs to hold onto his self-esteem/she needs him to talk to her so she feels competent—can make it very difficult for them to communicate.

Men recognize that there is a difference between how the two genders communicate. Women, however, often ascribe the dissimilarity to a man's lack of sensitivity. They don't realize that when a man distances himself, he's self-soothing in some way, attempting to build his masculinity and his confidence about his competency in the world.

Bear in mind, then, that when your husband is reluctant to tell you about his day, it's possible that he doesn't want you to know about a particular problem—a business crisis, a cash flow issue, or the loss of a major customer. He is not yet sure how he is going to deal with it and until he is, he doesn't want you to worry about it or give him advice. He would rather tell you about it once he has dealt with it.

Think of it as a performance issue for him. If he has to solve a problem, he doesn't want to spend any energy talking about it or trying to explain what's going on—that's a distraction which will get in the way of his feeling like he can take it on and solve it.

You can help him by letting him know that you understand that he is grappling with something, that his distance or preoccupation has nothing to do with you or your relationship. If you say something like, "You know what? It's okay. I'll give you space," the support that he will feel from your recognizing where he is, that he's not trying to be elusive or move away from you, will help him solve it. Then he will be able to come back to you and discuss the problem and how he solved it without feeling like he also has to fix the damage that was done between the two of you.

While your husband has his independent focus—"I've got to make sure I can keep performing, and that I'm good at what I do,"—you have your own performance issue: You keep the universe spinning. You have to take care of everything—your family, your husband, the family business, perhaps your own career as well. You may be thinking, "I've got to make sure he can do that, I've got to make sure that everybody else is taken care of and I've got to make sure that I'm doing what he is doing in my own career." Adding to your stress is that while you are feeling all of that, perhaps hyper magnified, your husband is doing his independent thing at a distance from you.

SETTING LIMITS

Your husband may express his frustration and fears indirectly. He may obsess about something he read in the paper, or what happened on the golf course over the weekend or how he suddenly can't stand the cat. He may become a hypochondriac. If a minor cut on his hand isn't healing fast enough, he may be sure that it's cancer. Or he may ask you at dinner, seemingly out of the blue, if you still love him (a signal that he is afraid he is about to lose everything, and that he does not want to go through that alone).

It may take weeks, but eventually you will find out what is really bothering him, at which point, realizing that it had nothing to do with you, you will undoubtedly breathe a sigh of relief.

Or he may express his worries more directly. He may tell you that he wants to downsize your life style; to move the family into an apartment in a peaceful little town in the middle of nowhere, where the rents are lower, and he can be more certain of paying his bills. What he is really saying is that he wants less stress, that he doesn't want to have to be on all the time, to have it all together.

When he suggests that you move to Podunk, in the midst of dealing with all of your own stress, you get scared to death. "Why is he throwing me this curve ball? Why doesn't he have his act together?"

Sometimes, instead of empathizing with him, it is actually more effective to set a boundary. You can tell him that you understand that he is doubting his own capacity, but you will not tolerate his self-doubt. You can say, "That's a cut. You fell on the ice. That is absolutely not cancer." Or "We've been to Podunk three or four times in our minds already. We've lived through that every single time. I'm not interested in having that discussion again. Let's move on." It may sound harsh, but what you are really telling him is that you believe in him, that he will get through this cycle or this crisis. It may not be the immediate response he was looking for, but in the end it's the one that will best serve him, you, and your family.

My husband does not accurately assess the talents and weaknesses of the children who are working in the business. How do I voice my opinion?

Whenever you and your husband talk about your children who are about to, or already have, entered the family business, your respective genders, priorities and positions relative to the business will likely affect your differing views. Mostly likely you want your children to be loved and treated equally, while your husband's focus is on the performance and how that should be responded to fairly.

As natural as it is for you to protect your family's harmony, when you express that intention vis a vis the family business, it can create a significant problem. Children working in the family business are held accountable at a much higher level of performance than they ever have before. When they were students, they may have been forgiven for less than excellent grades— "I know you got a C, sweet heart, but next time go for an A." Once they enter the business, however, they are in a performance arena which doesn't allow for repeated C's and D's and F's. The focus of relationship management is how to get the job done. If it were otherwise, the business would suffer, as would your children, who cannot grow without being held accountable.

A DELICATE BALANCE

In order to talk productively about your children's talents and weaknesses, it would be useful for you both to figure out how to assess their performance clearly, fairly and objectively. What are the criteria? What are the standards? What are the performance expectations? How can you know when they are being fulfilled? Are their job descriptions and functions clear? How do their positions compare to "industry standards" in terms of title and compensation?

Putting a traditional business matrix on job descriptions is not the only way to evaluate the appropriate compensation for your children. Family businesses have an unwritten rule: "We take care of family," which manifests in different ways. Your husband, as a family business owner and member, has a certain amount of privilege and leeway. Once you and he have made performance criteria objective by creating job descriptions and functions that make sense for what your children are doing in the business, you can be creative in how you meet your family needs, and how you attain family harmony, adding compensation where you want. In other words, you can find the delicate balance between holding your children accountable through objective criteria and maintaining family harmony.

SEPARATING APPLES FROM ORANGES

Frank and Sally, who are retired, built a chain of sporting goods stores. Their older son, Stephen, currently runs the business, makes all the major decisions and acts as the business's visionary. Through good times and bad, Stephen makes sure that his parents and his younger brother, Michael, who also works in the business, have their income. Stephen owns sixty-five percent of the stock. Michael manages one of the stores, earns a salary that is almost twice what it would be were he not a family member, but owns no stock.

Sally is focused on family harmony, specifically, her sons' relationship. She believes that Stephen is stepping on Michael, and that Michael is entitled to some of the remaining stock. Stephen already makes more money than Michael, who has also committed his life to the business and is an asset to the company. She also believes that Stephen doesn't give Michael enough credit.

Frank, on the other hand, is focused on his sons' performance, and is making judgments about what is fair based on that. He believes that Stephen is being very generous to Michael, since he's overpaying him for his skill level; he could hire a twenty eight year old to fill Michael's job, while Michael would not be able to find another job that would pay him anywhere near what he is making.

How do Frank and Sally resolve their differing points of view?

The first step is to understand that they are fighting for different things, with different priorities, but that they both have valid points of view and reachable goals.

The second step is for Stephen and Michael to substantiate clearly and unemotionally what their respective roles are. Once they articulate how they each contribute to the business, they are more likely to respect and appreciate each other, which in turn will help them resolve issues of control and compensation. They can then talk about whether or not Michael is being overpaid and how he can share the responsibility of risk more equitably

In terms of the stock question, it's not unusual for the sibling who enters the business first, who has the more entrepreneurial spirit, i.e. makes the decisions and takes the risks, to get the bulk of the stock. But if Michael, who also lives and breathes the business, agrees to carry some burden of risk, he can make it easier for his father to give him some percentage of the remaining stock, which is what Sally is bucking for. Should Stephen wish to be the sole owner when he faces the question of succession, he can even buy Michael out. In sum, as long as the parents separate out business issues from family issues and the brothers communicate, Sally, Frank, Stephen and Michael can find a number of ways to solve their problems.

> You can find the delicate balance between holding your children accountable through objective criteria and maintaining family harmony.

THE PERIL OF COLLUSION

In the following family, once again, the father is performance oriented; and the mother is more focused on the relationship between her children, but their problems are more complex and far harder to resolve:

After Alice and Harvey retired from their family real estate business, their older daughter, Susan, and her husband, Ed, continued to work in the business, as did their only son, Kenny. Ed was always highly effective but he was also emotionally and psychologically overbearing towards Kenny, who was not much of a worker. Alice and Harvey had two other daughters, both younger than Kenny. One worked outside the business; the other was a stay at home mother.

Because Kenny was their son, Alice and Harvey were never able to come to terms with his weaknesses. They compensated him commensurately with Susan, a much harder worker. Although they didn't accept Ed's behavior towards Kenny, they liked that Ed generated a lot of money. Comfortable with their cash flow, they were never able or willing to resolve the tension or to make a decision about who would eventually end up with what stock.

Kenny is now in his fifties, and Susan and Ed are close to sixty. Recently, Harvey died and Ed became terminally ill. Alice, influenced by her two other sons-in-law, decided to split the stock among her four children. Unsurprisingly, Susan feels betrayed by Alice's decision. She and Ed worked their entire adult lives for the family business and were never able to get any kind of footing. Not wanting to spend the next twenty years of her life making her brother and sisters rich, her only alternative is to sell the business.

The primary source of the family's problem is that Kenny never wanted to work in the family business. He was forced into it by Harvey, who believed it was Kenny's responsibility to work in it. After refusing to pay for Kenny's college tuition, Harvey disapproved of Kenny's poor performance in the business, not realizing that Kenny was acting out his anger at his father by not performing. For a man, independence is the root of self esteem. Kenny felt emasculated for years.

The parents' failure to assess honestly Kenny's talents, weaknesses, and desires, and to respond accordingly, underscores the importance of original placement. Alice colluded with Harvey. They both remained in denial about the consequences of forcing Kenny to work in the business. Worse, they let the conflict fester unresolved for thirty years. When they were ready to pass the business onto their children, the issue came back to haunt the whole family.

THE LURE OF DISTRACTION

Frequently, parents' inability to acknowledge and address a child's problematic behavior is a sign that something is wrong in the marriage. Rather than deal with a difficulty in their relationship, parents allow their child's negative behavior to serve as a distraction from it. As a result the child comes to believe, albeit unconsciously, "If I continue to act out, my parents will stay together rather than confront their own issues." In clinical terms, he becomes the "Identified Patient." What he is actually doing is signaling a dysfunction in his parents' marriage.

Any time there are unresolved core problems at the heart of a marriage, those issues are going to splatter all over the walls of the family business. In that light, think about the following difficult questions: When you state that your husband does not accurately assess your children's talents and weaknesses, are you saying that you do? Is it your husband's fault alone? Have you managed your child in a way that has proven to be successful? How long has the problem existed? Have you and your husband figured out how to work together to have your child perform?

> When you state that your husband does not accurately assess your children's talents and weaknesses, are you saying that you do?

OPPORTUNITY, NOT A RIGHT

Both mothers in the above examples believe that their sons have certain rights because they are children in the family business. While children in a family business may eventually acquire assets from it, they should not automatically have the right to work in it. Parents can create estate plans through which they share their assets—the monies their business generates, their wealth—among their children, but they ought to differentiate between sharing assets with their children and offering them employment in the business.

It is one thing to give your child a job in the business if he needs one. It is another to move him into a management or leadership position for which his only qualification is that he is a family member. If your child expects to work in the business, you can manage his expectation by talking to him honestly, so that he has the chance to adjust to reality sooner rather than later. If you postpone the discussion about reality for too long, a chasm can develop between expectation and reality and create a huge problem.

One facet of reality to share with your child is that as a family member he will have a leg up in terms of opportunities within the business, but he will also face disadvantages. For one thing, he will be working under a microscope. His every little error will loom large. In addition, he will be wedged between the employees and the family. Non-family employees will approach him with complaints about events in the business; and since he has to keep his relationship with other employees harmonious, he will not know what and what not to share with you. That is a very difficult position to be in.

THE IMPORTANCE OF CLARITY

The more you and your husband agree to treat the business as a performance arena in which preparation is everything, the more productive your discussions with your child will be. Similarly, the clearer you can be in terms of creating structures, the better off your child will be when he does enter the business. Being proactive about creating routines through governance structures or through accurate job descriptions is very helpful. If your child is already working in the business, you and your husband can discuss how to create sensible structures with appropriate boundaries. Everyone performs better when they know what's expected and what the rules are.

points to remember

If your husband resists talking to you about the business or is upset about something at work and won't share why, don't take it personally and don't give up.

Men and women really are different in how they think, behave, feel good about themselves and communicate.

When you set a limit for your husband, you are actually encouraging him: You are telling him that he is capable of achieving his goals as a businessman, husband and father.

It is possible to find the balance between creating objective criteria for your child's performance in the business and maintaining family harmony.

There's a difference between granting your child the automatic right to work in the business and giving him the opportunity to do so.

Things go best when there is consistent communication between you and your husband and between both of you and your child.

chapter two

IMPROVING THE QUALITY OF YOUR LIFE

I'm worried: My husband does too much and is under too much stress.
Most likely you're worrying that your husband's stress level could affect his health. If he got sick, or worse, died, you would lose him and your relationship. Although the thought may not be uppermost in your mind, you're probably also worried that you wouldn't know what to do about your own situation or the business, especially if you don't know what's going on in it. If you've been urging your husband to slow down and he doesn't listen to you, here are five reasons why your pleas may be falling on deaf ears:

1. He has always been this way. As an entrepreneur and owner of a family business, your husband has doubtless been a highly energetic, hard worker for decades, most likely since you met him. His work ethic created habits which he has held onto for decades. Old habits die hard.

2. The business is his identity. Your husband's definition of himself depends upon where his identity is banked. If it has been banked within the walls of the family business until now, he will have a hard time redefining himself.

3. He needs to know he can still "cut it." Your husband's ego, emotions, and independence come from the idea that he can still perform effectively. Where else besides the family business is he going to get that confirmation? On the golf course? Traveling? Unlikely. As long as he remains immersed in the family business, with all its stresses and worries; as long as he is still making important decisions, he will continue to experience himself as vital. He does not want to give that up. That is why we read about highly successful CEO's of family owned businesses who, nearing eighty, insist on deciding how a fourth floor bathroom should be decorated.

4. He doesn't want to admit that he's getting older. To one extent or another, we all choose to deny the reality of aging. We look at recent photos of ourselves that we don't like, and our first thought is that the picture didn't come out well—there must have been something wrong with the camera or the focus or the angle—instead of acknowledging that we have simply gotten older.

5. He's overcompensating. Although your husband may notice that it's a little harder to get out of bed in the morning, or that a muscle hurts in a way it hasn't before, he is still driven to feel as good as he did in his 20's and 30's. He doesn't want to know that it's harder to lift something, or go all day without a break or deal with five problems at once. In order to stave off the sense of helplessness that accompanies aging and to prove that he's not losing strength, he may go into overdrive and do more, rather than less. And he's not necessarily conscious of it.

While your husband may be grappling to have some control over his life, you may also feel that you have no control—over *his* behavior. However, there are things you can do:

1. Attend to Basics. You can encourage your husband to get regular medical check ups, and not to miss appointments. You can prepare healthy meals. If he notices that dinner seems different and asks, "What is this?" you can reply that you both need to change how you eat. If he needs to exercise more, you can find ways to do it with him, whether that means playing tennis with him or taking long walks together.

2. See the Bigger Picture. Conversations about planning for the future or about aging are not easy to initiate, but they are important. The best time to address those issues is when your husband is in his mid-50s. During that time, when children are leaving home, and bodies are changing, we all tend to become more reflective. The notion of mortality starts to feel a bit more real—hence the term "mid-life crisis." This period is a window of opportunity for the two of you to talk about how you want to spend the rest of your lives.

The conversation will become harder to have by the time your husband is in his 60's. By then he's more apt to focus on the thought, "I'm actually going to die." That thought, along with other negative associations, will make it much less likely that he'll want to talk about the future or to plan for it.

Once you are able to engage your husband in a conversation about getting older, you can point out that aging is part of a natural progression; that the challenge facing you both is how to adapt effectively. Bringing up the subject will heighten his level of awareness.

3. Follow through. You can be the one to implement the changes you both agree upon. You can be creative in terms of building leisure time into his schedule, whether that means traveling or boating or starting any other kind of hobby through which the two of you can share time, interaction and intimacy, assuming, that is, that you and your husband want to spend time together. If you don't—if you married each other "for better or worse, but not for lunch"—then the quality of your relationship has somehow been compromised. In that case, you have two options: You can do the things you enjoy by yourself while your husband continues to work harder than is good for him; or you can do your best to improve the quality of your relationship.

Will we ever be able to take the time to enjoy the fruits of our labor?
You have watched your husband work hard for years. You have done everything you were supposed to do. You have raised your children. You have been a steady, consistent support to him and his role in the business. You think the time has finally come to buy that condo in Palm Beach or take that trip to Paris. Your husband, however, cannot switch his focus from working long enough to talk about it, let alone to commit to it.

If this situation sounds familiar, it doesn't mean that you have to wait around, unable to make any kinds of plans because of your husband's need to stay planted in the business. Here's what you can do:

PLAN A: STATE YOUR CASE
You can tell your husband that you understand that he lives and breathes the business because that is who he is, but you still want to spend time with him and share your life with him. You can point out your concern

Stating your case to your husband may threaten him, but it may also help him acknowledge his mortality.

that by the time he is ready to devote less time to the business (including overseeing the new decorations on the fourth floor bathroom) one of you may be too old and/or sick to go anywhere or enjoy yourselves. Express what makes you happy and fulfilled. If you want to spend time in a condo in Palm Beach, whether it be sitting on the beach, joining a bridge club or doing some decorating yourself, let him know that you want to go there, even if it means being by yourself some of the time, and that whatever time he can spend there would be wonderful.

Stating your case to your husband may threaten him, but it may also help him acknowledge his mortality. The thought that he might have only ten or fifteen years left may prompt him to ask himself questions, such as "What is it all about?" "What have I been doing with my life?" "Am I truly happy and fulfilled?" "What matters most to me?" Most likely he will realize that he what he cares about more than anything is his family and that part of the reason he has worked all these years is his sense of responsibility to them. At this point in his life, the best way to serve them may no longer be by continuing to work hard every single day, if by doing so, his wife, children, and grandchildren don't see him or spend time with him the way they want to.

PLAN B: DO IT ANYWAY

If your husband doesn't respond to conversations about what you want for yourself and your relationship with him; if he still cannot tear himself away from the business to spend quality time with you, you can go anyway. If it is something you want, need, have earned and deserve, think about taking the trip to Paris or renting the condo in Palm Beach, even if it means going without him. It is not that you want to create a crisis in your family; you are looking for a way to get your needs met.

By being proactive and not assuming that it's all up to your husband, you are once again setting limits. In the same way you told him that you weren't moving to Podunk when he doubted his capacity to succeed in the business, or when you informed him that you were cooking differently because you both need to improve your diets, you can let him know that you are researching condos in Palm Beach. It is another way of saying that you are moving on.

If you are daunted by the prospect of behaving so assertively, recall who you were when you first got married. By and large, successful men marry strong, independent women because they don't want to worry about them *and* the business. The two of you probably started out on an equal footing. Over time, as you took on the role of wife/mother/care taker, your sense of autonomy may have dissipated. If you say to your husband, "Hey, the heck with you. Guess what? I'm going to Palm Beach," it will remind him of the person he originally married. He will remember how much fun the two of you once had, and he will want to have it again.

In the end he will most likely follow you. How many weekends will he remain alone, working and working? He will get lonely. He will think, "I'm coming home to an empty house, while my wife is enjoying herself without me. What am I doing up here?" And once he takes the plunge and buys the condo, it will be an asset he won't want to waste. Once he shows up for a weekend, he'll think, "What's so bad about this?" And with today's technology, he can stay in touch with his business through his blackberry. He can be obsessive and crazy if he wants to, but at least he is with you.

The Family Business is the Mistress with Whom I Can't Compete.

The family business may consume so much of your husband's thought, attention, and passion—demanding that he travel a great deal, miss dinner when he is in town, or work late into the evening—that you feel as though the business is stealing him from you. You may even believe that his commitment to the business is greater than his commitment to you and your family. How do you remedy this state of affairs?

CHANGE YOUR PERCEPTION/CHANGE YOUR ATTITUDE

You may not be able to change your husband's relationship to the business, but changing how you view the situation may change your attitude towards it.

The character traits that first attracted you to your husband are most likely the very things about him that now drive you crazy. Among the reasons you married him may have been his determination, discipline, focus, ambition, competence and commitment to success. Now, some years later, those same qualities keep him at work—and away from you—more than you would like. Try this: The next time your husband frustrates you because he has trouble shifting his focus from work to home, tell yourself that that you married an excellent provider, and he still is one.

You could also remind yourself that you and your husband *both* wanted him to succeed. Whether you helped your husband build the business from the beginning, or you married him when he was already working in a family business, and you knew he might be its CEO someday, his decision to work in or run the business was most likely not thrust upon you. You probably agreed to it, supported and valued it. All benefits come with burdens. Your husband's commitment to the business has brought you the house in which you live, the food you eat, the clothes you wear, the vacations you take and the schools your children have attended. The stability of your life, the environment in which you have raised your children, the values and sense of responsibility you have been able to impart to them are all by products of his success.

While your husband is primarily work oriented, your focus, whether you have a job or not, is more than likely taking care of the social aspect of the family. Both roles are critical. Competing about who is working harder or who has a longer day can get you into trouble. After spending the day car pooling, helping your kids with their homework, refereeing sibling squabbles, preparing meals, keeping the house in order so that your environment is livable and pleasant, all the while managing the myriad crises that can crop up in a single day, you probably don't appreciate the question, "What did you do all day?" Your husband, who has spent the day working hard in order to provide for all of you, would also like to be valued for his efforts.

GET INVOLVED

Perhaps, in the early days of the business you and your husband shared the common bond of building the business. While you had little or no money (and possibly no children) you may have done the books at home, gone to the plant with him or helped with whatever needed to be done to get the business off the ground. If so, you felt involved, vital to the success of the business. But as the business became financially stronger and/or when you had young children, a shift likely occurred. If your focus turned to the home, the commonality of the work experience may have diminished. You may have become less up to date on the events in the business or felt that your husband's life was more fulfilling or exciting. Feeling isolated or excluded can fuel resentment towards the business you once built together. One remedy for your isolation is to figure out how to get yourself involved in it:

Carleen was a stay at home mom with three children. Her husband, Doug, owned and ran an import/export business which took him to South America five times a year for three weeks. The combination of his frequent traveling and daily involvement with the business left him virtually no time for Carleen, not even for sex. (Talk about the business being a mistress!) Their marriage deteriorated. Although they didn't get divorced, they lived separate lives, like proverbial ships passing in the night.

Carleen figured out how to rekindle their relationship: She went on the road with Doug. She discovered that when he wasn't burdened by the daily demands of the factory, he was more relaxed and fun to be with and more available to spend quality time with her. They never went out to dinner or a play at home; but when she started going with him on his extended trips, they ate dinner together every night. Although he sometimes entertained guests at dinner, other times they had dinner by themselves. Sometimes they went to a play. Lo and behold, their sex life improved.

The quality of their conversations improved as well. During the time they spent at the airport and on the plane, Doug would explain to Carleen the goal of the trip, how he was accomplishing it and what the pitfalls were. The more Doug included her in his thoughts about the business, the more important her comments and advice became. As a result, Carleen became more confident. Understanding that sometimes she would be striking out on her own, she became adept at working side tours into the trip. Taking the time to plan the social components of those trips opened a whole new world to her. She found a way to take care of her own needs, her husband's needs and the business's needs without feeling resentment.

Carleen's decision to participate in her husband's business life greatly improved her marriage. She had to accept a division in her life—what her marriage was like when Doug was home versus when they traveled. That arrangement might not work for everyone, but it worked for her.

If, like Carleen, you do not work in the family business but you want to connect to your husband and to know what is going on his life, you too can accompany him on a business trip—it doesn't have to be to another continent.

You can also create social situations in which to meet your husband's trusted advisors, lawyers, accountants and other business associates, all of whom have an enormous amount of information. In a social situation, a trusted advisor and an entrepreneur are bound to talk about the business. When an advisor sees you sitting next to your husband at dinner, he will assume that your husband trusts you and will therefore share information easily. Once you have established a connection, you can express your worry that the business is consuming your husband to an unhealthy extent. Since you are both members of your husband's support system, you can use the advisor as a kind of translator for you. He may be able to voice your concern in language that your husband will hear and heed.

FILL YOUR OWN WELL

Women give a lot in terms of energy and time during the course of their day. If you are not seeing your husband as much as you would like or if he is not participating in family life enough, especially if you have small children, your reservoir of energy will naturally get depleted. Once that happens, it becomes hard to do anything well. Rather than blame your husband, who is also exhausted by the end of the day, or look for him to make you feel better, which will likely lead to conflict, you can take care of yourself. Carve time out for yourself, whether that means going to the spa, reading a book, exercising, or gardening—whatever nourishes you. Once your needs have been filled, not only will you feel better, it will be easier to attend to other's needs, including your husband's.

While it may seem to you that your husband is in control of his life and able to satisfy his ego through his work and success, the truth is that if he is heavily involved in his business, he is working that hard to take care of you and your family. His intentions are good. He does

Carve time out for yourself, whether that means going to the spa, reading a book, exercising, or gardening—whatever nourishes you.

not think that he is depriving you of fun. He has to go to work—kill that bear—in order to provide for everyone else. If he is knocking himself out at work, he may well believe that he is doing more than his share. He may experience a level of self-sacrifice, and if he does not feel appreciated, he may have his own resentment. You can help him by urging him to take better care of himself. If he does, he will be a happier camper when he comes home.

THE CHALLENGE OF MARRIAGE

Fifty per cent of first and second marriages in the United States end in divorce, as do eighty per cent of third marriages. Despite those statistics and the doubt among many that men and women are even capable of monogamy, couples still enter the age old institution of marriage hoping and intending that they will live a long and happy life together.

What happens? When things go wrong in one way or another, spouses fail to communicate effectively and become distant from each other. They cope in a variety of ways. Some have extra marital affairs. Some drink too much. Some become workaholics. Some do all of the above.

Both husband and wife focus their attention on their spouse's coping mechanisms without realizing that they are symptoms of unhappiness in the marriage—certain needs are not being met. Who is responsible for meeting those needs? They both are. First, they each have to admit that they are in an unhappy situation; then they have to see what they can do about it. They each have to ask themselves if it's possible to resolve their conflicts. If it isn't, then they have to decide whether or not they are going to sacrifice the rest of their lives to an unhappy marriage or whether they want to work on the marriage. Either way, they have to take responsibility for their decisions.

Marriages succeed not because both people are happy all the time, or always get along, but because both parties persevere. Marriages in a family business have an investment not only in their personal relationship and history, but in the business as well. Those couples know that while divorce is difficult under any circumstances, the consequences of divorce in a family business are enormous. Having agreed upon how they are going to survive in the world, they are that much more motivated to work things out. They know that achieving a successful marriage—like any kind of success—takes work, commitment and perseverance.

points to remember

Having perspective on why your husband does "too much" will enable you to step back and assess areas where you can gain control and have constructive input.

Communicating your concern to your husband as part of a larger conversation that he does too much will help you move forward as partners into the next phase of your lives.

Rather than waiting for your husband to change his habits, you can think about ways to change the situation. Sharing those ideas with your husband is a way to state your needs.

If you have been waiting too long to enjoy the "fruits of your labor," if you act first and take care of yourself, your husband will most likely follow.

Remind yourself that you supported your husband's success from the beginning and that you still benefit from it.

Finding ways to know more about the family business can reduce your concern that your husband is overly involved in it.

Take care of yourself by filling your own reservoir.

A successful marriage takes commitment and perseverance.

chapter three
PREPARING FOR SUCCESSION

How do I get my husband to step down and let the children run the business?

It's wise to start thinking about succession as early as your 30's and 40's. Complex legal/financial issues as well as family dynamics require time for adequate consideration, discussion and resolution.

Some questions to think about: What strategies will you use in dealing with formal questions of estate planning, legal structures, legal documents and the like? How are you going to prepare your children to take over the business? How will you navigate through the emotional issues that may surface between your husband and your children? How will you discern what in the end will work best for the business?

THE QUESTION OF MATURITY

Before your husband can or should step down, it would be wise for both of you to assess not only whether your children are competent enough to take over the business, but whether they are also mature enough.

> Victor, age seventy-five, owns a car dealership. His son, Andrew, has been in charge of it for ten years, during which time he has tripled its business. Andrew is eager to quadruple, even quintuple the business—he would buy four more companies and merge them if he could—but Victor, who is dependent upon his son for his income, and no longer making decisions about

how that income is generated, is afraid of the risk involved.

Victor lets Andrew take a lot more in salary proportionately than he does. He is even willing to give him 90% of the income and take only what he needs to live on, but he will not relinquish his 51% of the stock. Before he lets go of what he did for forty years, turns that 1% over and gives Andrew control of the business, Victor needs to be sure that he is doing the right thing at the right time. He still needs Andrew to prove that he can skipper the boat.

The car dealership sells Volvos. Every two years Victor gives everyone in the family a new Volvo. Andrew insists on driving a Porsche. That undoes Victor, who believes you must drive the car you sell. Andrew's response: "Having tripled your business, I will drive whatever car I want."

On the one hand, by stepping down from his day to day responsibilities without relinquishing that 1% of stock to Andrew, Victor is not dealing with the reality of an eventual buy-out or estate tax payment. He is putting Andrew in a position where he will have to buy his father out twice. Does that make sense? Is that in every body's interest? As the value of the business appreciates through Andrew's efforts and not Victor's, is it fair for Victor not to share equity of ownership of it now?

On the other hand, Victor's doubts about his son's readiness to manage the business have some justification. Whatever his personal preferences, Andrew is making a terrible business decision by not driving a Volvo. In fact, it is not a business decision at all. It is a family decision, reflective of a family dynamic between him and his father. Perhaps Andrew, angry at Victor for not turning over the stock, is rebelling against his father. If that is the case, Andrew is undercutting himself by bringing a family decision into the business, where it doesn't belong.

While numbers are critical, they are not everything. Before he is ready to be in charge, Andrew has to get beyond the adolescent issue of parental control and accept his father for who he is, what he has experienced, and what matters to him. Any succession process becomes difficult if the next generation does not have sufficient empathy for what the senior generation is going through emotionally by giving up control.

DIFFERENTIATING RELATIONSHIPS AND ROLES

Fathers and children are always going to have subordinate/dominate relationships. Within the family that dynamic never changes. However, as the succession process takes place in the business, that relationship has to evolve into a partnership between the senior and next generations.

Partnering with a father in the business to get a job done has a different dynamic from the parent/child relationship within the family. Keeping those dynamics separate requires considerable finesse and skill, but it's effective. If Victor, for instance, in the role of partner rather than an authority figure, were to say to Andrew, "You know what? You need to drive the Volvo," Andrew could more easily hear and respond to the comment as a business opinion rather than an order from his father.

As the wife/mother in the family business, it is helpful for you to separate business issues from family matters and to discern, regarding performance requirements, what is in the best interest of the business. Driving a Porsche instead of a Volvo has nothing to do with what's in the best interest of the family, but it certainly has something to do with what's in the best interest of the business. If you were Andrew's mother, you could say to him, "If you want to drive a Porsche down a country road, fine. Do whatever you want. But when you are working every day, drive a Volvo." Similarly, if Victor always worked on Saturdays, and believed that Andrew should, too, and if Andrew were to ask, "What does where and how I spend my time have to do with my performance?" you could support your husband by explaining to Andrew that he needs to make the appropriate business decision.

CORE VALUES

Core values are innate to the success of any business. They are particularly important in a family business where values extend from generation to generation. Part of the struggle during the succession process is making sure that core values are made explicit and acted upon from one generation to the next. Conflicts arise when there is a discrepancy between the values of the founding generation and those of the next generation. The resolution of conflicts lies in reviewing those values and reaching a consensus about how to operate accordingly. Once values are agreed upon, discussions about any aspect of the business—whether it be driving the car you sell, working on Saturdays or making decisions about compensation—can turn a long debate into a two minute conversation.

My husband is the brains. What will happen to the business in our financial future?

Whether you have had an active role in the family business, an invisible but powerful one behind the scenes or have sat on the sidelines and left the running of the business to your husband, you share a rarely verbalized, nearly taboo concern: *With the transit of the business to the next generation, am I assured that my financial security will continue?*

If, until now, your tendency is to support your children in terms of their family relationships, and your husband's is to demand performance from them in the business, your attitude may shift as you worry about the business's ability to survive when your husband retires, becomes disabled or dies, and how that eventuality will impact your own financial future.

Not having the same level of confidence in your children as you do in your husband is normal. Having raised your children, you naturally feel more comfortable being in charge of them than you do being dependent upon them for your financial security.

PUT YOUR OXYGEN MASK ON FIRST

Intuitively, women want to protect everyone else first—their husbands, partners, children, parents and grandchildren. A cornerstone of any estate and succession plan, however, is to make sure that you, as a member of the older generation, are provided for. Taking care of yourself first will give you the freedom to protect those you care about, without worrying whether or not the financial success (or lack thereof) of the younger generation will affect your ability to live your life independently.

Navigating the maze of transiting the business to the second generation while ensuring financial security for yourself can be tricky. Take a cue from flight attendants: "Should there be a problem, first put your oxygen mask on and then put the mask on your minor children." In other words, you can only help your children be successful if you take care of yourself first.

Too many women wait passively for someone else to plan for them. They count on their husbands or family advisors to understand the family and business dynamics and to identify and solve problems. Think about what that means: Would you leave the raising of your children to the school without any input from you? Would you allow your nanny, day care provider or ballet teacher to raise and influence your children

without your involvement? **In other words, you**
Why, then, would you allow **can only help your**
others to plan your future **children be successful**
without your participation? **if you take care of**
Dealing with disability, **yourself first.**
death, conflict, uncertainty
and succession is not easy. It is
natural to postpone addressing these difficult issues until tomorrow. The
problem with that approach is that by the time that "tomorrow" comes,
it may be too late to plan. The die may be cast in a form that is not easy
to change. The time to be involved and to talk to your husband is *now,*
when your input can make a material difference.

If you are afraid of sending the message to your husband that you
are not sure whether he is properly handling the estate and succession
plan, a starting point for the discussion may be the possibility that if he
dies before you, he would be unable to be involved. You can express to
him that it is important for you to understand what will happen if he
becomes disabled or dies, that it is essential that he plan the succession
of the family business, which provides financial support to both of you
and to others in the family. It is important to begin the vital discussion.
While there is still time to change them, try to have answers to the questions which are highlighted on page 32.

Caroline was a traditional wife and mother. Her husband,
Harry, was a hard hitting, single minded businessman
whose grandfather had started the business. When his father
died, Harry bought his mother's and sibling's interests and
then went on to triple the business's net revenue. He went
to work early, came home for dinner (the focal conversation of which was always the business) and went back to the
factory at night. On many occasions he cancelled weekend
dinner plans with Caroline. She considered herself a "business widow."

Caroline had never had a voice in the business or been
involved in any estate planning, which had not progressed
very far, since Harry thought he was invincible. Her situation

How will succession happen?

Do you know who will be in charge of the family business? Is it one or more of your children? Do they get along? How solid is that child's marriage? Do you get along with your son-in-law or daughter-in-law? Do you know what will happen if something happens to that person?

Are you comfortable with your cash flow if anything happens? Who would you turn to for advice? Do you know who the advisors are now? Have you met them?

Do you know who will be in charge of your assets?

Is your financial security dependent on the health of the family business? Do you know what the risks are?

What types of agreements are in place to protect the business and the family assets and income in the event of divorce, death or creditor issues?

Do you have a vote in the sale or succession of interest in the business?

changed dramatically, however, when Harry, still in his 50's, was diagnosed with terminal cancer and given six months to live.

The whole family went into shock. After his diagnosis, Harry realized that he had to bring Caroline into planning discussions, particularly about their children's involvement in the business. The children had started coming to the office with Harry as soon as they were five years old. (He put them to work stuffing envelopes, licking stamps and packing boxes.) They were now old enough to be working in the business full time. Although they wanted to maintain what their father had worked so hard for his whole life, they were not yet mature or experienced enough to take over the business and run it.

Among the many issues facing the family, the first and most crucial was whether Caroline felt financially secure enough to give her children a shot at running the business without their father's involvement and mentoring. Fortunately, due to a combination of non business assets and Harry's life insurance, which, when invested, could earn an income for Caroline, she could maintain her lifestyle and still afford to put a plan in place which would give her children the room to try some version of the business.

The next issue was how Caroline, who wanted to give her children the opportunity to run the business, could protect her assets from becoming at risk, should there be a downturn in the business. Harry was adamant that Caroline not put her personal assets on the line for credit or loan purposes. A solution emerged over the course of several meetings: shrink the business to a line that would be easier for the children to maintain and grow, i.e., focus on the aspect of the business that had the best chance of surviving Harry's death.

Harry was realistic. He foresaw that commercial banks and lenders might not lend money to children with minimal business experience. Therefore, another key step was to put together an informal board of advisors to whom the children could turn when needed. The children also needed an exit plan, a way to determine when and if they should consider bailing. Harry believed that within a few years of his death, it would be clear whether or not the children were going to make it. Because the time frame was short enough, he had an idea of who the players might be for them to approach with the idea of selling, and whom they should avoid.

After sitting on the sidelines for her entire married life, Caroline was thrown into center stage. In deciding what position to take, she considered two additional factors: First, because of the estate tax factor, it was not economically prudent for the children to own the very lucrative business. Secondly, Harry did not have enough time to decide which child should be in charge—who had the talent to lead, and who would be fair to the family. (Ironically, although Harry had bought his mother and siblings out so that he could run the business without interference, he now wanted anyone who wanted to participate in the business to share in the benefit.)

Caroline made an interesting decision. She agreed to serve as a place holder. The business was put in trust for her benefit, and her children were named as trustees. She declined to come into the business, however, given that it was not her strength—she didn't understand it—and she wanted to give her children the freedom to make whatever decisions they thought right. Comfortable in the knowledge that she had enough financial assets independent of the business to live her life without relying on the success of the business, she remained on the sidelines and allowed her children to see what they could do.

The first lesson to be learned from Caroline's story is that if you're worried about what will happen to your financial security when your husband is no longer running the family business, it is important to find another way, through a combination of non-business assets and your husband's life insurance, to shore up your own financial future. If you do, any decisions about the business's future can be made independently of your own security. In other words, by standing up for yourself financially, you can afford to give your children the opportunity to run the business and the room to take the risk of losing it.

> By clarifying what mattered most to him, he strengthened his intention to protect his wife, children and business.

Secondly, Caroline and Harry made astute decisions about their children. Rather than burdening them with the pressure to keep the business successful into the second generation, they gave them the luxury to fail. By doing so they actually exuded confidence that whatever happened, things would work out. The business is still thriving.

How did Caroline and Harry act so wisely? In the face of death, Harry went to the absolute core of himself. By clarifying what mattered most to him, he strengthened his intention to protect his wife, children and business.

How can you and your husband reach that level of awareness, without being told that he has only three weeks to live? You can use your imagination: How you would feel in such circumstances? What would be your basis for decision making? What values would assert themselves?

If you can take care of yourself and still give your children the opportunity to succeed, whether they do or not, you can rest easy. And if they do succeed as a result of your decisions, the pleasure you will experience is the best in the world.

A FATE WORSE THAN DEATH

As difficult as it is to plan for your husband's death, planning for his disability, cognitive or physical, is even harder. While death brings closure, and allows surviving family members to move on, emotionally and behaviorally, disability can perpetuate a crisis indefinitely if things have not been put in place beforehand. The loss can be so painful that in order to protect themselves against it family members are apt to deny it. Their emotions are so powerful that they rise above their ears, rendering them incapable of acknowledging reality or of moving beyond it.

When the person in charge is no longer capable of making decisions, but is still alive, a huge vacuum occurs in the absence of his authority and complicates matters. Who becomes the decision maker? How does a family gather and create a new decision making system under the stress of a parent who is at risk or disabled?

When William, who had started his family business, a chain of department stores, had a stroke, his wife, Sarah, and her son, Phillip, who ran the business after his father became disabled, still looked to William both for his approval and to make decisions, even though William was incapable of providing any answers. While a non family business would find a way to move forward, William's family froze. They continued to act as though William were still the decision maker, even though he no longer could or even wanted to be.

Sarah was responsible for perpetuating the holding pattern. William had set compensation for Phillip at a certain point in time; and even though Phillip had taken on a lot more responsibility since then, nobody would change it. Sarah could have stepped in as an authority figure; but she did not agree with how Phillip was running the business or how he was treating her two other children, another son and a daughter. Instead, in order to balance out the children's dynamics, she kept William "alive." As long as the children deferred to him, she continued to have leverage. She allowed the family dynamic to act as a checkmate to Phillip.

Sarah cared about her family and the business, but she had no road map for taking steps to ensure its success when William was no longer able to run it. That situation changed only when the family sold the business and divided everything equally. Although the business sustained its value during this hapless period, the family members wasted many years of their lives.

How do you avoid what happened to Sarah and her children? How do you prepare your children for the eventuality of your husband's disability? In addition to acknowledging the loss of your husband as the active decision maker, it's important that your family appreciate the consequences of owning a family business and be prepared to deal with them. The wisest preparation would be to formulate a plan, including an alternate decision making system, so that your family dynamics will not undercut the business's ability to function effectively should your husband become disabled.

points to remember

The succession process involves addressing legal and financial issues, your children's readiness to be in charge of the business and your family's dynamics, all of which are best handled with awareness and care.

The most effective way to distinguish family decisions from business decisions is by maintaining best business practices.

The core values of your family business can act as a useful frame of reference for resolving conflicts.

When you plan for succession, as much as possible, imagine the perspective you would have if you were facing death or disability immediately. The more you can do that, the wiser your decisions will be.

The best way to anticipate your husband's inability to run the business, due to death or disability, is to make sure that you have other systems in place.

PART II

mother

As the core of the family, a mother has a powerful impact on the family business. To the extent that she raises her children to take responsibility for their actions, she can make an extraordinary contribution to the business. Likewise, any family dysfunction in which she plays a role will also express itself in the business.

chapter four

TREATING YOUR CHILDREN FAIRLY

My husband is often harshly critical of my child for underperforming in the business. What can I do?

If your husband is too critical of your child's performance, the harshness of his criticism may make it impossible not only for your child to perform well, but also for you to manage your own emotional response. It may be too hard to remain neutral, to find out more about what is going on or to discern whether your husband's assessment is valid or an overreaction.

If asked to side either with your child or with the business, whether or not you have seen your child's performance, your instinct will be to pick your child—a mother will always be a mother to her cubs. However, as counterintuitive as it may feel, it is important for you to choose the business first, not because the business matters more than your child, but because s/he needs to live up to certain standards and perform at certain levels for his/her and everyone else's benefits.

THE NEED FOR ACCOUNTABILITY

Before your child enters the business, it is important for you and your husband to talk about what values you want your child to learn by working in it, the most critical of which is accountability. If you and your husband have been holding your children accountable all through their lives, continuing to do so in the family business will not be a big stretch. If you have not raised them that way, although it is still not too late, it will be more difficult to start holding them accountable in the family business.

Part of teaching accountability is having a child face consequences when he does not perform up to standards. Protecting him from those consequences will undermine his growth. Not only will he continue to under perform, he will impact negatively on his father's relationships with other family members who work in the business and on the morale of other employees who will notice the lack of consequences for his inadequate performance. It would be better for everyone involved if you would point out to your child that having chosen to work in the business, he should now live with the consequences of that choice, including working with his father. Without that limit, he will continue to stir up issues, and will continue to pit you and your husband against each other.

Sometimes a child's inadequate performance is a result of a limitation or problem, for which his mother excuses him from being held accountable. Considering him a special case, however, will only feed the mother's protective instinct and incline her to allow him a broader base of acceptable behavior. Having little faith that he could make it in an outside company, she might even feel that the family business is a good place for him to hide.

Any child who goes into the family business, however, regardless of skill set or intellect, can make some kind of contribution, even if s/he will never rise up within the organization. S/he also needs to be held accountable for his behavior. Not doing so is actually a form of disrespect, since it implies that s/he does not have the capacity to improve him/herself in any way.

THE TENDENCY TO TRIANGULATE

Sarah believed that the family business should take care of her son Ted, who had a childhood history of battling ADHD and struggled with self esteem. She continually pressured her husband, John, one of three brothers in charge of the business, to give ownership of it to Ted, even though he wasn't yet ready for that kind of responsibility. Ted in turn depended on his mother to fend for him and negotiate with the father for his position.

John was a workaholic. Consumed by the family business, he was never at home or available to his wife. As a result, Sarah, angry and resentful that her emotional needs for closeness and reciprocal nurturance were unmet by her husband, developed an overly intense relationship with her son (who was also very good at getting Sarah to go to bat for him). Pointing to the years of sacrifice she endured as a result of John's absence from home and his role as a father, Sarah demanded that Ted have whatever leadership role he wanted in the business. She even threatened John with divorce if he did not succumb to her and Ted's wishes.

Ultimately, John gave into Sarah and gave Ted his shares of the business prematurely. John's decision created tension between him and his two brothers. They asked to sell their shares in the business and left it in the hands of John and Ted. Lacking a strong relationship or effective communication skills, the father and son were ill equipped to run the business effectively. Furthermore, Ted lacked the depth of experience necessary to support future succession.

Although it was not Sarah's intention to sabotage the business, her need to rescue Ted undermined it and set the path for his failure. If she had not pushed John to take care of Ted through the business, John's brothers would have stayed in it, and Ted would have had the opportunity to develop through performance metrics established for him in the business, thereby increasing his chances of success.

The root of Sarah's overprotective behavior was her relationship with her husband, John. Even in good marriages, it is not unusual for spouses who are both working hard in their respective roles to become too exhausted to meet each other's needs. Conflicts can surface when they each think it is their turn to be nurtured. They may lose touch with each other; their relationship may suffer. Their problems, however, can usually be overcome through constructive communication.

A deeper family problem develops when one spouse, feeling neglected or angry, turns to a child to get his or her emotional needs met. The family then becomes "triangulated." The child is not only a surrogate spouse emotionally; he or she becomes a third party through which both dysfunctional parents communicate indirectly with each other.

The lesson here is to be careful about getting your emotional needs met through your children. Sometimes a child wants to manipulate the situation to his or her advantage and will encourage the triangulation. Other times the child more innocently wants to take care of the mother, who can then take advantage of the child's need to please her. As tricky as it can sometimes be, it is important to set down appropriate boundaries, to remain the adult in the relationship and to allow your child to remain the child. In order to perform your role as a mother appropriately, remain aware that major issues with your husband can compromise it. If triangulation does appear, look first at your relationship with your husband.

Are my children being treated fairly, whether they work in the business or are stockholders?

"Treated fairly" can mean many things: that a child be given sufficient opportunities to grow and learn things in the business; that evaluations of a child's performance are objective; and that the father look at his child neutrally, unclouded by the child's early history, if that has been troublesome.

Most commonly, however, "fairly" is thought of as "equally," i.e., all siblings should receive the same compensation. Clarifying roles or functions in the business and referring to industry standards can help determine appropriate titles and salaries.

Evaluating management positions can be more subjective and complicated. Parents and siblings often feel that it is fair for family members in management positions, who come together to make decisions for the company, to be compensated equally, even if they do not all work the same amount. Doing otherwise would cause too much discord.

Determining fairness in terms of ownership or stock holding is a more quantitative calculation; but challenging questions still arise about who should have what—whether, for instance, children who do not work in the business should also have stock capabilities.

In the end, the answer lies in what each family has to do maintain harmony.

PLACEHOLDER POSITIONS

Parents often hold positions as a kind of legacy for all of the siblings who wish to work in the business. In instances where there is a wide age gap between children, some parents are reluctant to make a decision about who will end up running the business until the youngest child has had his or shot. The oldest sibling could be thirty, for instance, working in the business for five years, while the youngest is twenty and still in college. The parents might not want to lock anyone into positions and functions until everybody has had the opportunity to show what they can do, especially if they believe that the youngest is the most talented. Because a place has been held for him or her, s/he could eventually pass the older sibling. At the same time, a non-performing older brother or sister can remain in his or her position and hold the wheel of the ship without making any significant changes or additions to the business.

Another question that can arise is how best to assess fair compensation and stock capability for the child who has been working in the business for several years compared to the one who is just entering it. If the structure and size of the business allow for it, one answer is to create clarity in terms of roles and functions and then assign compensation and stock accordingly. In a smaller, less developed business, where roles are less distinct, parents may decide to pay all siblings equally, especially if equal pay for all is a value of the family. The parents may also differentiate compensation from stock, determining salary by function and dividing stock, which they view as a family asset, equally among the children.

Are those who are not in the business being handled in an estate plan?

You and your husband might give stock only to your children who are working in the business or to all of your children. In either case, if an estate plan is to be successful, financially and in terms of family harmony, it is important to get your children's input as well as your attorney's guidance.

ALIGNING BENEFIT WITH BURDEN

The first possibility is that only children who are or will be working in the family business, and who will eventually become owner/managers inherit stock in the business; those who do not work in the business inherit other assets. For example, suppose there are two sons in a family—Adam and Billy. Adam works in the in the business. Billy does not. The parents may plan to give the business to Adam and comparable assets to Billy. The issue of fair versus equal will come into play when valuating the business compared to other assets since Adam has the burden of maintaining the value of the business, whereas Billy, who will get cash, does not. The goal then is to value the business to the least amount possible so Adam will pay the least amount of estate taxes.

Since nobody really knows what a business is worth until someone pays cash for it, the valuation of the business is a target toss. If the goal is equality, which is not necessarily the same as fairness, one has to minimize conflict by allocating the estate tax burden to the recipient of each asset, since Adam, who will pay the proportionate share of tax on the business, is the only one who has a stake in how it is valued. Billy, who does not work in the business and does not have to pay estate taxes on it, does not have the same stake.

To avoid conflict between Adam and Billy, it would be wise for their parents to align the benefit and the burden so that each son will pay taxes on what he inherits. Otherwise, equal does not mean fair, because Billy will think that the business is worth more, which will only increase the burden of the tax on Adam.

Figuring out how to align benefit with burden is part of the planning process. For example, Adam can buy life insurance on his parent's life, receive it, and then pay the tax from it. Or, if there is a provision in his state's tax code, Adam can pay the tax on the value of the business over a period of years. Billy, who is getting the cash, however, cannot do that. However the plan is structured, it can be very tricky, and in the end, fairness may not necessarily mean equality.

GIVING STOCK TO EVERY CHILD

After spending their lives building the wealth and value of their business, which is now their largest asset, some parents may want to divide the stock between all of their children, whether or not they work in the business.

That thinking has merit. Family members who are not in the business are likely to have just as powerful an attachment to the business. Having grown up with the business as well, they are likely to feel insulted and angry if they do not receive any stock in it. Their egos, identities, and connection to family have also been shaped by the business, even if they have never crossed its threshold. In their own ways, they have sacrificed just as much as the ones who choose to be in the business. They have also not received the benefits which running one's own business can bring—independence and freedom, for example—which are unquantifiable but need to be discussed. If they have decided to pursue another career path, albeit with their parents' blessings (not all parents insist that their children work in the family business) they may still feel that they should receive stock.

INCLUDING CHILDREN IN THE DIALOGUE

Arriving at a successful estate plan requires a dialogue among family members and between family members and attorneys. Both present and future conflicts amongst siblings cannot be resolved by a structure in which they have had no say. Siblings may try to live within it to the degree they can, but because it's not theirs and does not contain or reflect the dynamic between them, they will play around with it but will eventually not use it. If, however, a family and its attorney develop a structure that in some form incorporates children's thoughts and wishes, the children will take ownership over it, significantly increasing the chances that it will work.

An attorney can offer a family a number of options and see which one makes the most sense for everyone. If a plan works for some family members and not for others, they can talk about it until they reach a compromise. For instance, if your husband is used to running things and wants to make sure that things go a certain way, he can have the will structured so that the children will have to meet a stipulated number of times a year, with the advisor present; if they do not comply, there will be a consequence.

Whatever compromises are reached, your attorney can help you figure out how to achieve your family's goals and how to avoid pitfalls. More importantly, whatever its provisions, the estate plan will have a much stronger chance of sustaining itself if your children have been involved in the process. It does not matter how the stock is set up, whether family members get the same or different amounts of stocks. What matters is that they come to some agreement about how they're going to make decisions.

It's important to note that while structures can be both sound and complex from a legal and financial point of view, they derive from facts available at the time in which they are created, as though the attorney took a photograph of the situation and then built a coherent and practical structure from it. Families are more like movies than photographs. They change. What may suit a family's situation today may not work in five or ten years. And while the attorney's structure may in fact prevent or even eliminate future changes, it should also allow flexibility to accommodate how a family's dynamic might play itself out.

Family assemblies enable all of your children not only to have stock in the business, but also a voice.

FAMILY ASSEMBLIES

Family assemblies, which include family members who own stock, but who may not work in the business, help govern the function of the business. If those not working in the business are still actively involved and educated about it, they can give some level of comfort and reassurance that the business will go forward into the next generation.

Family assemblies enable all of your children not only to have stock in the business, but also a voice. The assemblies constantly educate stockholders and provide an arena for ample communication between those who are "inside" and those who are "outside." Through them, a kind of partnership develops among the family members in terms of how the business is managed. They all get a chance to participate in the growth of the business and the benefits, both economic and psychic, of continuing to be members of it. Even if they do not know about the profit and loss sheet, those who are non-managers still have the values, the vision and the sense of importance of what your family business might mean in your community. And they still know a lot about what makes your business successful in terms of its culture and its values.

If your business is not large enough to warrant governance, or family assemblies, your children can still be informed about what is going on in the business. For example, a family member who is in the business can send out a monthly newsletter, at the end of which he can invite family stockholders who are outside the business to call him or come in with any questions or concerns. The idea of communication between family members in the business and those outside it can be part of the dialogue

WORST CASE SCENARIOS

In some families, particularly when the parenting has been deficient, the level of conflict among children can be so extreme that there is no hope they will ever come to an agreement on an estate plan. For example, if the father/business owner has been an autocratic patriarch and the only force holding the family together, once he is gone, the conflicts among his children will only get worse. The siblings can easily end up in law suits against each other.

If you think that your children are so volatile that chaos will follow your husband's demise, your only recourse is to stipulate in the estate plan that no child be allowed to sue another sibling without losing his or her inheritance. Once that prohibition is established, you and your husband can possibly create some sort of workable structure.

If, however, because of family conflicts or for other reasons, family members cannot find a structure to which everyone can commit, then the best solution is for everyone to split the assets and go their separate ways. The decision not to carry the business forward into the next generation can be a relief and the healthiest choice in the long run.

How do we choose the next successor without destroying the relationship between the kids?

Below are two models for choosing the next successor. In either case, as with estate planning, the outcome will be more successful if members of the next generation are included in the dialogue:

ANOINTING THE HEIR APPARENT

In any family business, there is a component of anointment that does not occur in other businesses. Although the senior generation cannot know for sure how to judge the continued leadership of an heir, a father, particularly a traditional patriarch, may decide to put his oldest son in charge, especially if he seems the most qualified at present. The father's, or "king maker's" advisors then become the son's advisors, too. If the father has ruled the roost, his heir, imitating his role model, may believe that he is the next godfather. He will take care of the people under him in the way he believes he was treated. He will make decisions about what is distributable income, or what is to be rolled back to operating reserve, and how much information he is going to share with others, even when and if the business is to be sold.

From a family dynamics point of view, the anointment model is problematic. The idea of having one sibling as an authority over the other siblings is not sustainable. Lacking the authority that a parent has over his or her children, no sibling can police another sibling well. When parents anoint the oldest sibling, whether or not he is the best performer, it is crucial that they have the support of the other siblings. Otherwise, the family dynamic—and communication among siblings— will deteriorate.

APPOINTING THE BEST PERFORMER

You may decide that instead of anointing the eldest, you will choose the person whose performance makes him or her the best qualified to run the business, regardless of sibling rank, or even whether s/he is a family member.

The child most suited to lead according to a system of meritocracy, however, has to be able to do more than bring about the best profit and loss sheet. To be an effective leader, s/he must also have the support of his siblings. While businesses are outcome driven, the quality of the daily work experience matters as well. Essential components of success include both consistency and stability over time. To borrow terms from team sports, s/he has to promote "task cohesion" as well as "social cohesion." In other words, his or her leadership has to suit your family's dynamics and to express your family's core values.

COMMUNICATING ACROSS THE GENERATIONS

If your children have the opportunity to express their thoughts and feelings about the best business model going forward, you can include that information as you create a structure. You can also discuss your decisions about structure with your children, giving them some choices about what they want to accept or what they want to alter.

The dialogue not only helps to create a structure that your children can live with, the process of communication between your generation and theirs will also increase the likelihood that the business will carry its success into the next generation. According to a study of failures in family businesses, "Attributions for Family Business Failure: The Heirs' Perspective" (Family Business Review 9 (2) by Karen Maru File and Russ Alan Prince, the senior generation in those families interviewed claimed that the younger generation did not know what they were doing, while the younger generation said they were not adequately trained. The failure of either generation to take the responsibility or initiative to provide or ask for adequate leadership training is both a performance and a communication issue. Indeed, without proper communication between the generations, the leadership issue becomes irrelevant.

The largest legacy of a family business, more than its financial wealth, is the set of values that have existed in the family and in its culture. If your children are prepared with those values, attitudes and philosophy, their success will not depend solely on the success of the business. Whatever happens to the family business, they will still be equipped to succeed in life.

points to remember

It is important for you and your husband to discuss what values you want to teach your children through working in the business.

Over protecting your children, or not holding them accountable for their performance in the business is doing them a disfavor.

Unresolved issues between you and your husband can lead to an inappropriately close relationship between you and your child, known as "triangulation." The remedy: Address the problems in your marriage.

Fair does not always mean equal. While compensation can be differentiated and determined according to roles, siblings in management positions are usually compensated equally.

Although salaries can range according to function and responsibility, stock may be considered a family asset and distributed equally, whatever positions your children do or do not hold in the business.

Maintaining family harmony is the most important factor in making decisions about compensation, stock and what is "fair."

Whomever you and your husband choose as the next successor—either the "heir apparent" or another child considered to be the most capable—s/he must have the support of his siblings in order to run the business effectively.

A dialogue between you and your children will not only help create a workable structure for carrying the business forward; it can also educate and train the next generation in how to lead.

It is essential for your children to be included in a dialogue about your estate plan. Otherwise they will have no "ownership" or commitment to it.

Family assemblies or other forms of communication between children who work in the business and those who do not but still own stock in it, will contribute to the stability and future of the business.

In families where conflicts are irresolvable and members cannot agree on a viable estate plan, the best option may be to sell the business and divide the assets.

PART III

~~

widow

Given that the average lifespan of the American woman is 79, and the average age at which she becomes a widow is 55, today's widow can expect to live many years after her husband's death. The following questions delineate several key factors which can enhance the quality of those years, both financially and emotionally.

chapter five

THE IMPORTANCE OF ESTATE PLANNING

What preparations should I be making while my husband is still alive?

If your husband is willing, encourage him to create an estate plan. And when he does, it is important that you advocate to be named a co-Trustee. As an heir at law, a widow has standing as beneficiary, but her rights are different from those of a trustee or fiduciary. She has a right to the accountings and can object, but her objections usually have weight only in the most egregious cases. It is far better to have a seat at the table and a vote as a co-Trustee. It would also be wise to examine the plan for answers to the following questions:

> Who is in charge of my financial health if my husband dies?
> Who is in charge of my financial decisions?
> Who has the right to make those decisions?
> Who is giving me money?
> What are the terms upon which I receive money?
> Who has the authority to sell?
> Who has the authority to transact a business?
> Do I have a vote?
> What is my recourse?
> What is my children's recourse?

It is possible for a husband to object to naming his wife as co-Trustee of the estate. If, for instance, he thinks that she doesn't understand money, that she thinks it "grows on trees," he may want to ensure that she never has control over it and never touches the principal. Or he may fear that she will remarry and, being naïve, will fall under the influence of her new husband, who will take advantage of her; that she won't realize what is happening until it's too late.

His fears may be unfounded, of course. His lack of trust in his wife's ability to handle finances, as well as any other decisions she might make concerning the trusteeship of the estate, are likely to be more a function of his relationship with her than a function of who she is independent of him. Just because she spends money in ways which he does not approve of does not mean that, absent their relationship, she would not be able to manage money or would not be in touch with reality. Different circumstances elicit different aspects of people.

Commonly, everyone, including the entrepreneur himself, considers him invincible. With the world revolving around him and his often larger than life personality, it is hard for anyone to believe that he will ever not be in the picture. Accordingly, unless your husband wants to create an estate plan, it may be difficult to make him do so.

There are situations, however, in which he might be motivated to create an estate plan. If he were to become ill, he would be forced to pay serious attention to the consequences of his death and would be motivated to create an estate plan. He might also want to create an estate plan if he has a unique, irreplaceable skill.

> Ivan designs and produces one-of-a-kind stained glass lamps. His customers are high net worth people who pay a lot of money for his pieces. He and his wife were both worried about what would happen to his business and his unsold lamps, which would increase in value if he dies. His workers, who implement his ideas, don't envision them. Nor could they replicate them exactly. And anything they create would have significantly lower value.
>
> To complicate matters, Ivan's wife Betty is an Air Force pilot, a high risk occupation. If something were to happen to her, or if she were not available to deal with things if Ivan died, they don't know who would figure out what to do with the business.

An estate attorney can suggest incorporating several safeguards into Ivan's and Betty's estate plan: putting an advisory board in place; picking a gallery owner who would agree to show the remaining lamps if anything should happen to Ivan; and assigning family members to be in charge of capturing the value of the business.

As unusual as this particular situation may be, acknowledging a potential crisis increases the awareness of the importance of estate planning.

POST-MORTEM PLANNING

Many people think that once an estate plan is done, the work is over. It's not. Post mortem negotiation is both important and powerful. Sometimes, in fact, it is just the beginning. Recall the snapshot/movie metaphor: Estate planning is a snapshot; life is a movie. Whenever a family member dies and the widow looks at the estate plan, it is never right; it cannot be—there is no way to get it exactly right. The best of estate plans cannot account for future and inevitable changes. The law might change. The business might change. The people in charge and their level of competency in the business might change. Since the movie keeps rolling, as much work should go into post death planning as goes into pre-death planning.

If you have not been named co-Trustee, after your husband dies or becomes disabled, the other trustees usually have the right to appoint a co-Trustee, and you should negotiate for that position. If you do not feel your voice is being heard, having a lawyer or accountant advocate with you (not for you) can also be powerful. Since estate plan documents are often unintelligible to a layman, sometimes it isn't possible to understand everything about the plan while your husband is still alive. In that case, there are many things that can happen after death that would act as pressure points to make things workable.

The estate plan can actually be the vaulting point for a whole new life. Although entrepreneurs' lives may seem on the surface to be reasonable and normal, they are often too complicated to be fully contained within the estate plan. Internal and external influences and dynamics evolve over time. Once the entrepreneur dies, many aspects of his life that have never been talked about, whether they are secrets or highly charged subjects, suddenly rush to the top of the list of things that have to be addressed. The entrepreneur may have had a mistress. He might have had children out of wedlock to whom he gave money a long time ago or even promised a piece of his estate. They can show up and disrupt things, demanding their shares or authority. Indeed, the stuff of post-mortem planning is often a scenario straight out of a movie.

My husband's advisers treat me like a second-class citizen. They act as though they have the same authority as my husband.
While your husband is still alive and healthy, it is possible to incorporate as part of estate planning who the best advisors would be. However, since the ideal choice of those who are trustworthy and can answer important questions will change over time, choosing advisors is including them in that static snapshot.

It is also important to be aware of the difference between an advisor who acts as a supporter, who will help you decide what you want to do, and a caretaker, someone who will try to do everything for you. The difference can be subtle, but critical. There is an emotional component to the caretaker role that has a hierarchical aspect integrated into it. He feels that he knows best. Because he knows your husband's wishes, he will assume your husband's role in respect to the business. If he is a confidante of your husband, he may agree to take care of you and your family after your husband's death. Even so, he cannot have the same level of authority as your husband with respect to you and your family because it's not possible to recreate the marriage contract in that way.

George was a commercial real estate developer. Henry, his lawyer for thirty-five years, drafted George's will and trust and named himself as trustee in both. Before he died, George had decided that he no longer trusted Henry but he never did anything about it. After George's death, Henry told Catherine, George's widow, that she would not be receiving any income for two years. Only Henry, as the trustee had access to the trust records. Catherine, as a beneficiary and widow, was legally entitled to see the records only at certain intervals of time, usually annually.

Because she was never made co-Trustee, in order to get a foothold in this situation, Catherine's only recourse was to hire an attorney who was completely and independently in her corner, and who would have a seat at the table with her. But even Catherine's attorney could not get any information from Henry since he was the only one with legal access to the information.

After a year and a half of not having any say, Catherine still doesn't want to go to litigation. Not only would she have to pay for her attorney, Henry could defend himself with Catherine's money since he is the trustee. In fact, he bills Catherine for all the time he spends talking to and corresponding with her attorney. The only thing left to do is for Catherine's lawyer to put enough pressure on Henry until he comes forth with more information, since he does have fiduciary responsibilities.

As frustrating as this situation sounds, and as infuriating as Henry's behavior may seem, it is not necessarily the case that Henry is a bad person. Consider the psychological component: Henry may mean well. He may have fallen into the psychological trap of believing that as George's former confidante and anointed trusted advisor, he can best represent George's wishes. He may believe that he can understand and protect George's interests better than anybody else. George may have told him things that he never told Catherine. Henry is then behaving according to his interpretation of what ought to be done. He may simply believe, with no malice, that it is his God given right to be in charge.

Regardless of a trusted advisor's good intentions, it is essential, therefore, in order to protect yourself from an advisor who anoints himself as the trustee of the estate, to become a co-Trustee and to have your own seat at the table.

points to remember

In order to have a vote and a seat at the table, while your husband is still alive, advocate to be named in the Estate Plan as a co-Trustee.

If you have not been named as a co-Trustee, you can still hire your own estate attorney to have a seat at the table with you after your husband dies or becomes disabled.

Post mortem negotiation is both important and powerful. Sometimes it is the beginning of a new stage of estate planning.

chapter six
TO SELL OR NOT TO SELL

My husband's advisors tell me to sell the business. Even though I have no experience running it, I feel responsible to my husband's legacy to keep it going. I'm also not confident that I would get the full value of the business if I did sell it.

There are many examples of widows who, without formal prior experience working in the family business, take over the family business and are successful at it. The process often goes something like this:

Initially, she is in a state of shock and unsure what to do. She has only a superficial understanding of what is in the estate even though, because of tax planning and second to die life insurance, she usually has become owner of the stock. Although she knows the business is important, is familiar with a lot of the employees and has an idea of who are good and who are not, she has little or no understanding of its operations.

Because there is so much at stake, she resists following the advice of her children, who also tend to be at a loss. The advisors' opinion to sell the business is not congruent with her sense of obligation to her husband to continue it; nor is she confident that she will receive the full value of the business if she does sell it.

After some pondering and struggling, she decides to hold onto the business, albeit blindly, and begins to educate herself. After a couple of years, the business has hung on and survived, in most cases with the advice of a lot of people who are familiar with the business or with what she is experiencing.

By the fourth year or so, she has a grip on her businesses. Now she wants more than just to preserve it. She has ideas about how to make it grow and she begins to execute those ideas.

Over time she integrates the next generation into the business. And even though she has never experienced herself as a decision maker and has little previous knowledge about the business, by translating her life experience into the operations of a business based on values and how she thinks things ought to be done, her business not only survives, it thrives.

Despite her achievements, rarely does she look back and say, "Wow, I did something great." More likely she is extraordinarily modest about what she has done and wrestles with the same issues that everybody wrestles with when trying to figure out how to integrate the next generation to succession.

Miriam's husband, Louis, the owner of a large, successful research company, discovered that he had a terminal illness, with a life expectancy of between five and ten years. He decided that his salary and savings wouldn't be a sufficient amount of wealth to support his wife or children, so he came up with an idea about how to form a different business, which he started out of his garage. He put together a board of his best friends, all of whom had experience in business, who would help Miriam when she later took on the business.

In about three to five years, the business paid the bills, but was not yet thriving. When Louis died, sooner than anybody had planned, the advisors told Miriam, who knew nothing about the business besides what she had learned watching Louis, that she should sell it.

After taking about twenty four hours to think about it, she told the board that she was determined not to sell, that instead she was going to make it grow. Although she wanted all of her board members to stay and help her, if they chose not to, for whatever reason, she would accept their decision.

All the board members stayed and they all pitched in. The business is now going into its third generation and is extremely successful. Miriam's three sons, all of whom are in the business, entered it at different stages. The oldest, who was a teenager when Louis died, went into the business when he was twenty-one and later became the CEO. The middle son also had a significant position. The youngest son ended up replacing his oldest brother as the CEO. They are now transitioning to a non family CEO with a strong governance.

After her sons took over, Miriam, by then a grandmother, remained on the board as a kind of informal CEO. Her sons ran everything by her. She was very demanding in terms of ethics, and insisted relentlessly that their product be absolutely the highest quality imaginable. That standard of excellence, which was passed on to and internalized by the next generation, continues to be the core of the business's success.

Here's another, better known example of a widow who took over her husband's business:

Wanda Ferragamo, the wife of the famous Italian shoe designer, Salvatore Ferragamo, took over her husband's business when he died in 1960, at sixty-two. Wanda, twenty-two years younger than her husband, was then a housewife with six children. She knew about the business—she and Salvatore had been very close—but she had never worked before. Wanting to honor her husband, his dreams for the company and for their children, she took over the business as a kind of mission. The factory's technicians and administrators saw her through the beginning years as the head of the company, in which she now serves as honorary chairwoman.

Like Miriam, while her husband had the initial vision, Wanda brought the business to the next level. Her sons are now taking it to the next level again. Last year, for the first time in its 80-year history, someone from outside the family was brought in to run the business. Michele Norsa, formerly the chief executive of the rival Italian group Valentino, replaced Wanda, now aged 85, who has cut down her workload and prepares to pass on the reins. (*The Independent*, February, 2007)

What Miriam, Wanda Ferragamo and other widows who have maintained and built their husband's businesses have in common is that up until they took over their family's businesses, they were very much involved with caretaking and other domestic responsibilities. After the initial stages of grief and confusion, they rose to the occasion, allowing an aspect of themselves to blossom for the first time. They did things they had never done before, including traveling to where they have never traveled before. Their biggest worry became whether they should date again and how that might affect their relationship with their children.

If I decide to keep the business, what potential problems should I be aware of?

Some widows, whether they keep the family business or sell it and become the matriarchs of the wealth and the trustees in a post-liquidity context, have trouble assuming the role of an authority figure. They are uncomfortable making tough decisions or holding the next generation accountable. They are afraid to confront their children for inappropriate behavior, or their advisors, for fear that it will impact their relationship with them. Frequently they use a male trustee or advisor as an authority figure. Not only does that not work, it upsets and angers everyone even more. The advisor may try to assume a level of authority that is essentially parental, without permission to be a parent. His advice, often personal, is experienced by the widow's children as intrusive.

Without the skill set or the constitution to risk confrontation, these widows invite chaos into the family. Their children fight amongst themselves, and in some cases, with their mothers, over their financial shares. If, however, the widow can muster the courage to assert herself and communicate her feelings, she can resolve the conflict enough to protect not only the stability her family, but also her own financial security, which should remain paramount.

Diane's son, Gary, had a terrible temper. When faced with a disagreement, he would go into an extended tantrum appropriate for a two year old. He would send insulting emails to her and to life long advisors, accusing them of dishonesty and of being utterly disappointing. Even though it ate her up, Diane acquiesced every time and gave Gary his way.

After three years of this, she finally decided that for the sake of her own health, self esteem and well being, she had to address Gary's behavior, even if there would be hell to pay and the situation wouldn't improve. She understood that her role in the dynamic between her and Gary was her inability and unwillingness to assume the authority role, even though she was the only one who could fill that role.

In a respectful way, Diane told Gary how upset and embarrassed she was by his behavior and that she couldn't take it any more. Gary's response was to tell Diane his side of the story, and together they were able to address unresolved historical issues between them. The result of their communication was much more positive than Diane had imagined it would be. She and Gary are now on much better terms and are able to express their mutual love and respect for each other.

Diane's decision to confront Gary reveals what can happen when one family member takes another family member seriously enough to talk to them honestly—it can open up a productive dialogue. Conversely, the most disrespectful thing one can do to another family relationship is not to be honest. Mustering one's courage is crucial since allowing fear to inhibit honest communication only creates more distance and increases the likelihood of losing the relationship altogether.

GETTING STUCK IN THE GRIEVING PROCESS

Losing a loved one is difficult in any case and brings forth strong emotions. Losing the founder of the family business and its and the family's decision maker has its own issues, which can express themselves in several ways. A widow and her family, for instance, can be so unwilling to lose the connection with the founder and father that they leave his office untouched, as though it were sacred ground. They may leave a big picture of the founder on a wall, imbuing the office with his presence. When the family begins to use the vacant office for meetings, they are

Mustering one's courage is crucial since allowing fear to inhibit honest communication only creates more distance and increases the likelihood of losing the relationship altogether.

signaling that they have begun to move on or that a succession process has taken place

Another indication that the family is stuck in the grieving process is that they cling to an old decision making process, even when, absent the key person in the process, it no longer works. When problems arise, as they inevitably will, the next generation is left scrambling without a mechanism to solve them. Family members may feel abandoned and resentful that the person who held things together has died. At the same time, they resist developing a new decision-making process because that means acknowledging the reality of his death. Until they do, they are unable to address the problems facing them.

In order for family members to work together harmoniously, it's essential for them to work through their grief, both individually and collectively:

On the surface, Norman was a wonderful husband and father who could be extraordinarily charming, loving and caring with his family. Unfortunately, he could also be unpredictably volatile. He had been physically and verbally abusive to his children when they were growing up.

Norman fell ill and was sick for six years before he died. When he finally understood that he had about six months to live, he decided to live the best life he could. As a result of addressing issues of life and death, he saw the world differently. He acknowledged and took responsibility for his history. His character and personality changed. How he talked to people changed.

During that time, Rhonda and their, son, Alan, both spent an inordinate amount of time with him. As a consequence of spending time with Norman in his enlightened state, they were able to work through all of the negative history they had had with him.

The younger son, Sidney, however, was so upset at his father for deciding that he would rather die rather than struggle with more interventions that he refused to spend any time with Norman. He left the family for the last four months because it was just too painful for him to be with his father.

Consequently, whereas Rhonda and Alan became much more settled about Norman's death, Sidney is stuck in the grieving process and continues to act out the historical dynamics. Because he is in a different place from his mother and brother, he is unable to connect with them or work well in the family business with his brother.

KEEPING UP WITH TRENDS

The grieving process can take years. During that time rapidly changing trends in the marketplace may occur which family members do not foresee or adapt to quickly enough. Three years is not a long time to deal with a sudden death of the family business owner and its practical ramifications. It is, however, a long time for new trends to emerge. Having an independent board of directors and non family members active in the business can help prevent that situation.

Ellen was a stock holder in her husband's printing company after he died. Her son and daughter ran the business. After three years, on the advice of her accountant, Ellen sold the stock and the company to her children and took a note back. The arrangement worked for a while. Ellen was not involved with the day to day running of the company but she maintained her cash flow.

The printing industry was changing rapidly and Ellen's children were not on the curve of those changes. (For example, no one buys five color brochures anymore. Everything has become digitized, and equipment is totally different.) In addition, Ellen's children were not as talented as their father had been or as apt to take risks, especially with their mother's money. Within five years, Ellen's children could no longer pay the note. Since Ellen didn't own any stock, she had no leverage. Not wanting to foreclose against her own children, she had the note restructured to make it more viable for the business by allowing for lower payments to her over a longer period of time.

Restructuring the note worked because everyone got along. But it remains a difficult situation for all of them.

Ideally, Ellen would have made sure that her husband left her with enough liquidity and assets separate from the business to keep her from being financially dependent on her children's ability to run the business and to foresee changes in the industry.

points to remember

If you're able and willing to assume an authority role, even if you've never worked in your husband's business before, you can translate your life experiences and skills into continuing, if not improving upon, the business's success. It can also be an opportunity for you to blossom.

Whether you take over the business or sell it, in order to protect family harmony and your financial situation, it is important to be in charge and to confront your children or advisors when appropriate.

After your husband dies, your family has to go through a natural grieving process, individually and collectively, before you can work together successfully and develop a new decision-making system.

Grieving can take years; new trends emerge quickly. If possible, keep up with industry changes.

chapter seven

MOVING ON

What should I think about if I want to date and eventually remarry? How do I bring it up with my children? If I do remarry, how do I protect my family and my new husband?

Dating is a healthy sign that you are moving on. Marriage, on the other hand, is a life-time commitment and ought not to be entered into as a reaction to grief or loneliness.

How you approach the subject of a new relationship or a potential mate with your children depends in part on how old they were when their father died. While you should be clear that it is your life to live, you need to take more care in how you handle the situation if you have young children than if they have already gone off to college.

The children's age relative to a new boyfriend or mate is also a factor:

> Bonnie is an attractive, wealthy widow in her early forties whose husband left her with a huge fortune. Within a couple of years, she fell in love with Chuck, a good looking carpenter half her age who makes very little money. When Bonnie and Chuck became engaged, Chuck moved in to Bonnie's house. Although Chuck is an affable fellow and is more interested in Bonnie's life style than in actually getting his hands on her money, Bonnie's children are distraught. They have not only insisted that Bonnie do a pre-nuptial agreement, which she should, they also have tried aggressively to break up the relationship.

Regardless of the ages of the parties involved, integrating someone new into the family is not easy. Children rarely want their parents to marry someone new.

points to remember

Dating is a healthy sign that you are moving on with your life.

Marriage ought to be entered into more carefully and should include the drawing up of a pre-nuptial agreement.

Integrating a new person into the family has to be done with great care.

PART IV

stepmother

A wise woman becomes a stepmother with her eyes wide open. The more aware she is of the challenges she faces, the more able she will be to take care of herself emotionally and financially.

chapter eight
SETTING REASONABLE EXPECTATIONS

I feel like an outsider. How do I get my voice heard?

A stepmother's role is extremely challenging. Although no two situations are alike—people's weaknesses and strengths differ, as do relationships—one thing remains constant: You will always be at a disadvantage. You may know a lot about family issues and have a lot of family responsibilities, but you will have absolutely no influence. If you attempt to give advice or to intervene in a particular situation, your input will not only be unwelcome; you run the risk of being rejected and characterized as an impossible woman.

Like all women, the stepmother wants everybody to "play nice" in the sand box. If and when they don't, she is inclined to help solve everybody's problems and make the family situation better. If that sounds familiar, you will soon find out, if you haven't already, that your desire to rescue everyone is wishful thinking. Once your rescue fantasy evaporates, the reality of how little control you have over the relationships in your blended family is bound to frustrate you—human beings like to control things.

To alleviate continual disappointment, try to remind yourself constantly that divorce creates loss for everybody, and that loss inevitably produces emotional conflicts. Create reasonable expectations of how much harmony you can or cannot create. Lastly, accept that there will be moments in which you will be included and moments in which, no matter how badly you would like it to be otherwise, you won't be.

CO-PARENTING

Children are more likely to develop into autonomous, healthy and successful people when both mother and father work together to address their children's issues. It is usually impossible, however, for the biological father and the stepmother to co-parent in the same way as two biological parents. For one thing, you may have a different approach from the biological mother to what is and is not permissible. Since your stepchildren are used to their biological mother's rules and parenting style, it will be difficult for them to adjust to a new set of rules and expectations. All you can do, for the sake of your own sanity, is to back up the rules of your house as much as you can.

It may be possible to co-parent or discipline very young children in a blended family. Even if your stepchildren spend time at another house, you can still create co-parenting boundaries with your spouse. ("In this house, this is what happens.") Once children are adolescents, however, you may be a support person, cheering for them from the sidelines, but you cannot be a mother figure who sets limits for them outside of her house, or with whom they share their deepest confidences. When they behave in ways that drive you crazy or make choices that you think are unproductive or irresponsible, rather than interfere, take a few deep breaths, acknowledge the limits of your influence, take a long walk and/or put your attention on something more positive and over which you have more control.

MONKEY IN THE MIDDLE

In those inevitable moments when your expectations are frustrated by your husband's decisions and behavior, you might find it helpful to look at things from his point of view. Like a monkey in the middle, he is pulled in many different emotional directions with as many competing allegiances. He has to navigate between you and his children from a previous marriage and between two sets of children if he and you have children together.

To manage his stressful position, he employs a variety of strategies. Sometimes, glossing over all the complex dynamics between his children and you, he chooses to view the situation through rose colored glasses, hoping that everyone will simply get along. Since he loves everyone involved, why can't they love each other?

At other times, without exactly lying, he opts not to tell everyone everything. He may not tell you anything that he thinks will upset you. He might even keep the children from his first marriage from meeting or having anything to do with you. If they work in the business with him every day, he may lead a kind of double life, keeping what he does during the day separate from what he does with you and your children.

> Like a monkey in the middle, he is pulled in many different emotional directions with as many competing allegiances.

Among the emotional burdens he carries is the guilt he feels about the impact of divorce on his children. He feels terrible about some of the events that have transpired in their lives—including his not being in their lives more—which have made them unhappy. Because of that guilt, he is inclined to overcompensate, both in how much he gives them and how much he tolerates certain of their behaviors. If they work in the family business, he likely has a difficult time holding them accountable, rationalizing that if it hadn't been for the divorce and the issues it created, they would be more responsible at work. Taking so much responsibility for his children's inadequate performance, he is inclined to cut them slack rather than punish them.

Not holding children accountable, however, fosters a sense of entitlement that is unhealthy for the children, the business and him. You probably have little difficulty noticing your stepchildren's sense of entitlement or how they manipulate their father. It may seem at times that his commitment to his children is stronger than it is to you, that because of his acute sense of responsibility to them he is sacrificing his relationship with you.

If you express that sentiment to him, his response is likely to be defensive: "What do you expect me to say? That I don't love my children? You knew when you married me that I had children and I was committed to them." He may explain to you that as hard as it is for him to say to you, "Look these are my children, this is important, and you need to live with it," it is that much harder to express to his children his commitment to you and the children you may have with him.

Rather than compete for his loyalty, a more practical approach would be to tell your husband that you understand his position; that you respect his efforts to establish his priorities as both husband and father. You can acknowledge how difficult it is to balance both priorities. If you have a respectful dialogue with him, your husband is more likely to understand your feelings while remaining clear about his intentions to fulfill his commitment to his children. And hopefully, he will be honest with himself, keep a personal score card of his dual roles and learn that while fulfilling his commitment to his children is not negotiable, it is not the same as overcompensating or not holding them accountable.

It is possible, if your husband honors his separate commitments, for all the parties involved to grow sufficiently to reconcile eventually in some form and have adult relationships. In the end, however, like you, your husband has little control over how all the people in his family system get along, including his ex-wife, (whom he may never completely write off no matter how she behaves) since it is up to everyone involved whether to reconcile or not.

NATURAL ENEMIES

Because a woman's self esteem is rooted in the quality and harmony of the relationships in her life, your natural inclination is to find a way for everyone to get along. You undoubtedly want your husband to be happy and to approve of your efforts to be a positive influence where you can. You want your stepchildren to be happy and to accept you. You even want the biological mother of your stepchildren to be happy and to accept you.

This last wish is the hardest one to fulfill and depends on how willing or able the biological mother is to get along with you. If she has moved on with her own life and is happy with it, there is some chance she will be open to reconciliation, thereby creating an opportunity for some degree of harmony. The situation will never be comfortable or anxiety free, but both of you might at least become capable of being respectful of one another and of behaving well in social situations.

Most likely, however, no matter how she feels about her ex—even if she has no affection for him whatsoever and wants nothing to do with him— she may be upset, envious and resentful that his current marriage is more successful, and that he is happier with you. It may seem to her that you are sitting on a throne, that you have everything that she wanted and still thinks she's entitled to.

Her territorial feelings are as natural and primal as a lioness whose cubs have been stolen by a female from another pride. And speaking of cubs, since she is the mother of your stepchildren, there are now two female authority figures in the family system, both of whom are interested in what happens to their respective children—a natural set up for competition:

According to a 2005 article in The *New York Times*, despite a "seemingly cordial relationship" between Wendi Deng, wife of media mogul Rupert Murdoch, and his former (and second) wife, Anna Murdoch Mann, the women's "conflicting maternal ambitions" clashed when Mr. Murdoch and Ms. Deng sought to change the trust of Murdoch's *News Corporation* to give their two young daughters, then ages 3 and 2, a greater role. However, the terms of Mr. Murdoch's and Mrs. Mann's 1999 divorce ensured that Mr. Murdoch's four adult children (three with Mrs. Mann; one with his first wife) would be the beneficiaries and trustees and that Mr. Murdoch could make no changes to the trust without their consent. The four children "…agreed that the trust could be changed to include their half sisters financially, but objected to their half sisters sharing control of the company."

Even if you and your husband's ex-wife do not conflict over a legal matter, if she is resentful of your position, her children, as a way of protecting her, will continue to act out in the system as messengers for her discomfort. Her unhappiness will find its way back to the father and you, dispelling any hope for overall harmony. In that case, don't blame yourself or lament the situation excessively; accept once again the limits of what you can do. Unless everyone works towards harmony, unresolved issues will continue to create discord.

STAYING CENTERED

Feelings of being an outsider will never completely subside. It's essential, therefore, not only to identify your center, but to hang onto it for dear life. Many things will threaten to throw you off: Sometimes your husband will get confused about his alliances and where they should be. He will make a poor judgment and get it wrong. Family business issues will arise. Your stepchildren will get manipulative, consciously or unconsciously.

Before your feelings of rejection escalate, identify, even become intimate with, the types of interactions or events that are apt to trigger your sense of rejection. Then, before those feelings get the best of you, talk to your husband about what is bothering you.

How do I assure that my children will be treated fairly in the family business?

You may be concerned about two sets of children: those you brought into the marriage and/or those you have had with your present husband. You may want all of them to have the opportunity to work in the family business. Marrying someone who owns and runs a family business, however, does not automatically give your children from a previous marriage the right to enter it.

Your stepchildren may also worry about what their father is going to do in terms of his estate—whether he plans to leave you what they believe you are not entitled to. Their fears can clash with your expectations for your own children and exacerbate an already complex situation. Any attempt to address highly emotional family issues will stir up the original loss. The resentment and anger attached to that loss will flow directly downstream to you, making matters only worse.

Nevertheless, some situations are more conducive than others. The age of your children is an important factor. If, for example, you bring with you a very young child, whom your present husband adopts, that child may be more easily accepted by your stepchildren, smoothing the way for an eventual entry into the family business. Even if a young child of yours is not adopted, if he starts working in the business as a teenager, part time or during the summers, he could then work his way up to entering the business and be accepted. If your child is older and he hopes to enter the business, he will be met with resentment by your stepchildren, particularly if they have already been working their way up in the business.

Another possibility is for your husband to keep things separate—for instance, to set up a separate business for your biological children. In that case, your husband would be treating your children equally in terms of providing them with growth opportunities, without bringing them into the family business with all the complications that can entail.

points to remember

If you are entering into the difficult position of stepmother, keep your vision clear and your expectations reasonable. Whatever your family's dynamics, your influence is limited at best.

Co-parenting your stepchildren with their father is very difficult, especially if the children are no longer small. By the time they are adolescents, the most you can do is be supportive and establish rules for when they are at your house.

Understanding and acknowledging your husband's challenges as the "monkey in the middle" will encourage him to appreciate your struggles as well.

Staying centered is crucial. When you experience feelings of rejection, before those emotions overwhelm you, communicate with your husband.

If you have children from a previous marriage, it is best not to assume that they have a right to work in the family business. However, if they are young enough to begin working in it part time as teenagers or during the summers, it is possible for them to enter it smoothly as adults.

chapter nine

MONEY MATTERS

How do I deal with my husband's assets? I have no idea what he is doing. As soon as he dies, his kids will take everything and I will be penniless.

If the family business is a significant part of your family's wealth, it's not a good idea to have your personal financial security wrapped up in it or to be dependent upon that once your husband dies. Getting stock will put you in a precarious situation because it will make you dependent on the business's cash flow.

In addition, when the wealth goes to your stepchildren, their biological mother, who has influence over them, will not be sympathetic to you. Even if the divorce was relatively amicable and she has moved on with her own life and doesn't wish you ill, she probably does not want to see you benefit. She will believe that her children deserve the primary economic benefit, not you.

TRY A LITTLE EMPATHY

Like most entrepreneurs, your husband may not be in the habit of talking about the business or his assets with his wife. If you are constantly worried and advocating for yourself or your children, you won't get the results you want. The more anxious you become, the less likely your husband will want to talk to you.

A more effective tactic is to make your relationship with your husband paramount. If you acknowledge the challenges he faces in the family and business and the difficulty of being the "monkey in the middle," he will recognize and experience that empathy and support. Your relationship can deepen sufficiently so that he may reciprocate. He may become more aware of your struggles as a stepmother. Feeling grateful that you have listened to him and supported him, he may want to figure out how to make sure that you are okay.

Since it's unlikely that your husband will initiate that conversation, it's up to you to do so. You can start with something as simple as "How was your day?" At first your husband may not be sure that he wants to tell you the truth. He might start by giving you a little piece of information and see how you respond. He might tell you something provocative, like his children gave him a hard time that day. If you say, "Right. I know. They are impossible," the discussion will end right there. But if you say, "That must have been hard for you," he may answer, "No. It wasn't that bad," and throw you another nugget. The process takes time and self-discipline, but it is worth the effort.

A more technical and practical approach would be to do a program like Quicken at home. You can enter all the household bills and revenue. If you command the family books, you can present them as a balance statement to your husband and start the discussion that way. Since men operate better working from mechanical tools, your husband may be responsive. Soon other questions will surface, including planning questions, through which you can discover more information.

You can also get involved in your husband's business life by getting to know his business advisors. They will appreciate your interest and share information with you.

What can I do to protect myself?

We have suggested that it is often effective for you to take care of yourself by taking a semi-passive role with your husband, guiding him through a series of situations, so that he opens up and sees you as someone to listen to and take seriously. However, if you cannot make progress that way, you have to do whatever else you can to take care of yourself. Living in a situation in which your financial future is uncertain is not healthy.

Entering marriage and a blended family from a purely emotional point of view can interfere with perceiving reality accurately—when it comes to business, for instance, a man says what he means. Hoping that you can win your husband over or that he will change his mind is deceiving yourself. Prenuptials are a better idea. Your husband may have

drawn up a prenuptial to protect him and his children. Why
not insist on a prenuptial that
guarantees you some financial
security as well?

Feeling grateful that
you have listened to
him and supported
him, he may want to
figure out how to make
sure that you are okay.

You can also have the husband take out a life insurance
policy and make it payable to
you, as long as he is insurable, and willing—you can't get life insurance on anybody else's life without his signature. Then, even if your
husband leaves all of his assets to his children, you are still protected.
You can also ask that the business pay the life insurance premiums,
since that is all you will be getting. If your husband dies before you
do, you can take your money (hopefully, several million dollars) and
be independent.

PUT A ROCK IN THE ROLL

Many founders of family businesses roll their wealth back into the company. If that is the case with your husband, one thing you can do is to
try to stop that roll, so that less than 100% of your marital assets get put
back into the business. If a portion of the wealth stays out of the business, you and your husband can build up your personal net worth. That
will make a difference later.

An interesting note: Florida is changing its law about income
earned. In many subchapter S corporations and limited partnerships,
the tax return will show more income than the founders actually ever
received because it gets plowed back into the business. However, income earned during the marriage will be considered marital property.
Therefore, when the husband/founder takes income that could go to the
family and reenters it into the business, one of the current issues, for alimony purposes, is whether that income should be taken into account in
determining alimony or child support. Even if a prenuptial agreement
separates out the underlying asset, does the wife then have a right to take
that accrued income and keep it off the table?

It's a volatile question that could be argued from both points of
view. On the one hand, it's not cash. On the other hand, it's building
somebody else's value. If, as a stepmother, you are not getting the share
in that business, your current marital income is benefiting somebody

else. Yes, while you're alive and your husband is alive you are both get-ting the fruits of that life style, but it's not going into your IRA or your Merrill Lynch account.

Even if everyone agrees that the income has to go back into the business for whatever reason, there ought to be some guarantee that you will get something, whether through a formal negotiation such as a prenuptial agreement, or an active ongoing discussion during the course of your marriage. The point is that you have made a valid contribution that could be seen as a sacrifice on your part.

THE FAMILY BUSINESS AS SYMBOL

Estate planning in family businesses brings up issues of control—who will run it, who will get its shares, etc. Family dynamics, including com-petition among family members for the father, get expressed in relation-ship to the business because at an emotional level the business symbol-izes him.

Perhaps, as is sometimes the case, the family business was built dur-ing the course of your marriage, with your input, energy and support. You and your husband may decide that you are joint tenants, each with rights of survivorship, i.e. whoever dies first, the other spouse gets the business or all of the stock.

The question then becomes what to do about your husband's chil-dren from a previous marriage, particularly if they work in the business. If the children get any stock, they also have some control and that can present issues. You may feel that those children don't work hard enough to deserve stock. On the other hand, if they work in the business, they are dependent on it, and the question will not go away.

The only thing you can do in that situation is to hire some very good family business consultants to help you balance out the emotional and business concerns. It is too much to expect that you can resolve those issues by yourself.

WOMEN OF INDEPENDENT MEANS

Like many stepmothers, you may have your own earning power. What you do with your own income or assets is also part of this equation, es-pecially if you are not protected by your husband's estate plan. You may have to think about increasing your own forced savings or find other ways to keep yourself independent.

Here is an example of how one woman took care of herself when the prenuptial agreement provided no security for her:

Sam made it clear to his wife, Thelma, from the very beginning that he wanted everything to go to his children from his first marriage. He never changed his mind. Fortunately, Thelma had an independent income. When Sam was later diagnosed with a terminal illness, he named Thelma as durable Power of Attorney. Thelma is now taking care of Sam, using his money.

Sam's children are objecting. They argue that the prenuptial agreement stated that Sam's money would go to them. They are only partially correct: They will get their father's money, but only when he dies. They are actually fortunate that Thelma is staying with their father and is willing to take care of him, even though he is not leaving her anything. She is being prudent not to use her own money to take care of him.

Not every stepmother is as realistic or independent as Thelma. But if you are in a blended marriage and family, you ought to know what you have gotten into and should set reasonable expectations. There is no one external solution, but you can set a boundary within the chaos of your blended family. You can define your own sense of peace.

As is the case with your mental and physical health, you cannot expect that your financial security will be created for you or that your husband will protect you. With his rose colored glasses, he may not be able to conceive that you are not protected. If he were forced to tell the truth, he would likely admit that he knows that once he is gone, not everyone will live happily ever after. But then again, if he could admit that, he might not sleep so well at night.

point to remember

Financially, it's unwise to count on your husband's business to take care of you after he is gone. Whether through a prenuptial agreement, ongoing discussions throughout your marriage or your husband's life insurance policy, you need to find a way to take care of yourself.

PART V

daughter

The daughter in a family business faces both challenges and opportunities: She has to deal with the cultural bias towards women's roles in the work place, learn to communicate effectively with other family members and separate sufficiently from her father to become her own person. But she also has the flexibility afforded by the family business to create a fulfilling, balanced life as a mother and career woman.

chapter ten
YOUR RELATIONSHIP WITH YOUR FATHER

How can I improve my communication with my father? Will I ever get his approval?

If you have a hard time communicating with your father, it's most likely because you believe that he doesn't take you seriously. If you're stereotyping him as another man who doesn't listen well, you may refrain from telling him things he might actually want to know. You are much better off talking to him anyway, trusting—or at least risking—that he will hear you. Keeping upsets, concerns and burdens to yourself is unproductive and can undermine your ability to be successful An uncomfortable situation will not only remain so, the distance created by the lack of communication will make things worse.

In general, it's easier for a daughter to get her father's approval as a human being based on her level of happiness or the quality of her relationships than for her performance in the business or for other accomplishments through she which she may define her sense of identity. If your father's definition of your success is different from yours or from his definition of your brother's success—as it may well be—that difference may lead you to feel that your father doesn't accept you fully. The truth is, however, that approval or disapproval in any parent/child relationship has a lot to do with a parent's own history and ability to communicate affection and love. What approval means, after all, is unconditional love, which is a separate issue from how you perform in the family business.

In situations where the parent isn't particularly good at communicating unconditional love, children have a tendency to work extraordinarily hard, become very effective performers and high achievers in order to gain that approval. (One finds that a lot, for instance, in adult children of alcoholics.) The sad truth is that those children will never experience parental approval. That parent is never going to turn around and say, "I've have been waiting thirty-five years to say this: You're phenomenal." S/he doesn't have the capacity. Ultimately, both daughters and sons have to accept their parents' limitations, love them anyway, and find approval within themselves.

How can I get my father to give me more responsibility?
In the business context, it is actually easier for a father to delegate responsibilities to a daughter than a son, due to the underlying issue of competition between fathers and sons.

FATHERS AND DAUGHTERS VS. FATHERS AND SONS
Little girls are raised differently from little boys, who, as early as two years old, tend to be much more aggressive. While girls are more social, apt to play with each other, sit closer to the teacher in a class and pay more attention to stories, boys engage in parallel play—doing similar things near, but not with, each other.

Fathers also tend to show affection to their sons and daughters differently. They are gentler and more obviously affectionate with their daughters but play more vigorously with their sons, wrestling with them, or engaging in other forms of physical play. From a classically Freudian perspective, when testosterone starts to develop in young males, they have a lot of energy which they express in relationship to their fathers in a traditionally competitive, frequently very physical way, setting the stage for a competitive interaction later on.

Fathers and daughters are not so competitive. The lack of competition between them carries over into the family business, where a father is less threatened by his daughter's ambition or desire for more responsibility than his son's. He knows that a son, given more authority, might move toward independence, as men are wont to do, while a daughter with more responsibility will still maintain her relationship with her father.

A father also knows that a daughter rarely goes "outside the lines." As a woman, she pays close attention to relationships and will have more of a tendency to "ask for permission instead of forgiveness." If the

daughter feels she might alien-
ate or upset her father in any
way, she'd much rather repress
whatever needs she has in order
to maintain that relationship,
even if it means sabotaging her
own success.

> At the end of the day, women who succeed are those who appreciate what they're up against.

TALK THE TALK

A father is apt to be concerned about his daughter's ability to be successful in the larger business world, which, despite changes, is still very male-oriented. He will not be sure how effective you can be in aligning herself politically when most of the people you will deal with are men.

One skill you can acquire in order to improve your communication with men is the ability to engage in a performance dialogue, or "menspeak." In general, women tend to communicate about issues through narratives or long stories. They have a tendency to answer an e-mail with a long, drawn out discussion, several paragraphs in length, which includes examples of why there is a problem with something. In contrast, performance dialogue focuses on specific issues and remedies expressed in concise terms, e.g., the customer care problem was A, and the solution to it is 1, 2 and 3.

In the interest of securing and building relationships, it sometimes is appropriate to elaborate. But elaborating on a point can lose an audience and postpone problem solving. Not every interaction has to be explained. It's often more important to get to the task at hand, to be specific and clear in asking questions or making suggestions. Once you understand what a performance dialogue is, learn its language in the business context and engage in it verbally and in written communication, you can become much more successful.

At the end of the day, women who succeed are those who appreciate what they're up against. They learn very quickly how to assert and finesse their leadership and use their relational capacities to their fullest to lend trust. To put it simply, if you can get the job done, your gender will be unimportant. Despite the cultural barriers or biased perceptions challenging you, if you know what you are doing, people, including your father, will sense that and will give you a broad path.

points to remember

Rather than fear that your father is not willing to listen to you, try trusting that he is interested in what you have to say. Keeping your problems to yourself will not help the situation. It will only increase the distance between the two of you.

Receiving approval from your father has much less to do with whether you deserve it and much more to do with your father's ability to express unconditional love.

The lack of competition between you and your father, compared to that between your brother and your father, works in your favor.

Your father may have an easier time delegating responsibility to you because he trusts that you will still want to maintain your relationship with him and not become more independent, as sons are wont to do.

chapter eleven

FINDING YOUR PLACE

How do I deal with the reality that my brother is the implied successor? I'm more qualified and perform better than he does, yet it's assumed he's going to be in charge.

In patriarchal, "old world" cultures, women are often the workhorses, expected to do their jobs well, but not to have stock or voting power. The position of authority is handed down to sons, who are expected to take care of the family. In China and Japan, the oldest son is responsible for everyone—not only his own nuclear family, but his parents and siblings as well.

Cultures do not change easily or quickly. The idea of evaluating a woman's achievement in the workplace is still, relatively speaking, brand new. Consider the feminist movement in American history: Women received the right to vote only 100 years ago, after fighting for it, even going to prison for it. The second wave, what we call the women's liberation movement, is less than fifty years old.

How and when Katherine Graham (1917-2001) took charge of *The Washington Post* is an indication of how recently women's roles have shifted:

As Warren Buffet states on *The Washington Post's* website, "Kay had been taught all her life—wrongly—that only men possessed a managerial gene." The daughter of Eugene Meyer, former owner of *The Washington Post,* she worked for the newspaper from 1938 until 1945, when she left to raise a family. In 1959, when Meyer stepped down, he chose her husband, Philip Graham, to take over his position, even though Phillip suffered from bipolar disorder. (Meyer was blind to his son-in-law's illness, which manifested itself in numerous extra-marital affairs.)

Only after her husband committed suicide in 1963, did Katherine become the newspaper's publisher. She remained in that position until 1979. She was also chairman of the board from 1973-1991 and Chairman of the Executive Committee of the Washington Post Company until her death.

Because she was the only woman with so much authority many of the men in the company didn't take her seriously at first. According to Buffet, although Graham initially lacked confidence, her "brains, character (and) guts" led her to a "spectacular performance" which "far outstripped those of her testosterone-laden peers," both journalistically—The Pentagon Papers and Watergate occurred under her watch—and financially. The timing of her rise to power with the women's movement in the sixties led her to promote gender equality at the newspaper.

Contrast the obstacles Katherine Graham faced with Ivanka Trump's opportunities today:

Ivanka Trump, 27, is the daughter of real estate giant, Donald Trump. Like her father and older brother, Donald, Jr., she is a graduate of the University of Pennsylania's Wharton School of Business. After working in other business for a few years in order to gain experience, she became Vice President of Real Estate Development and Acquisitions at the Trump Organization. Not only does she hope, along with her two brothers (she also has a younger brother, Eric) to take over her father's business someday, her father seems to take her as seriously as he does his sons. "They have my ear," Trump said in *the St. Peters-burg Times* in 2006. "I respect them."

THE BIOLOGICAL IMPERATIVE

One cannot overstate how strong a part nature plays in determining a woman's role in the work place. The founding women in Israel's kibbutz movement, for example, were so aware of the impact that bearing children would have on receiving equal levels of labor assignments, respect and influence that they told the men they would have no children for five years. After that period, they negotiated as part of their agreement to have children raised in a community center by people who were assigned to care for them. Even those positions rotated so that a woman could also drive a tractor as part of her work contribution.

From our anecdotal experience, as a result of cultural pressures and the biological reality of motherhood, if there is a brother available and willing, he often has a better chance than his sister does of becoming the next CEO. No matter how competent, promising or hardworking a daughter may be, her father is likely to want grandchildren and to have his daughter raise them without the aggravation and burden of running a business.

Despite the odds being against you, if you want to compete with your brother for the position of successor, you can. Statistics back that up: Five percent of non-family companies in this country are held by women, compared to 25% within the family business. But you have to vie for the position of CEO carefully, thoughtfully and more subtly than your brother would. If you can connect with your father and engage him on matters that are important to the success of the business, he will be more inclined to trust you and include you as his eyes and ears. Because of your relationship with him, you actually have more flexibility in the family business, where there is more openness for definition of your role.

How do I balance having a career in the business with being a mother?

One could argue that women and men are treated relatively equally today in terms of their ability to get educated, acquire advanced professional degrees and enter the work force thus equipped. That equality shifts once a woman confronts the reality of balancing her career against parenting

You may be frustrated because it is nearly impossible to do either thing fully—work or motherhood. You may feel caught in the middle, earning less than your brothers but more than your husband. You can't go flat out for maximum responsibility in the business without sacrificing your role as a mother, and vice versa. You are probably primarily responsible for your children (babysitters and nannies aside). If you want to work full time and receive compensation equal to your brother's but still want to leave at four o'clock to pick up your children, he will probably not like that. On the other hand, if you decide to work only half time, it's likely that you will get stuck working three quarter time, at a minimum, if your responsibility doesn't decrease as much as your time does.

There has to be a give somewhere.

THE FAMILY BUSINESS AS SAFE HAVEN

Despite the challenge of combining motherhood and work, in comparison to other business settings, the family business has a lot more potential to be flexible. It can acknowledge your skill sets while allowing you to balance your work responsibilities against those at home. While expectations and subtle issues associated with the roles of men and women will not disappear entirely, you have a much better shot at negotiating a position that will be good for the business, your own nuclear family and the larger family as well. You are more likely to find a fair balance between hours spent working, compensation earned and fulfilling your role as mother.

So in those moments when you're frustrated that you can't "have it all," try shifting how you see your situation: You actually have the best of both worlds. You can be grateful that you can work in your family's business and have "a piece of the action." You are included in the family and still able to raise your children in a way that you feel is healthy. As long as you're comfortable with the balance you can achieve in your life and don't look to some external standard for validation, you can be satisfied, even appreciative, that your family business offers you the flexibility to both work and be a mother—a stock for which there is no price tag.

How do I manage my relationship with my siblings and keep things fair in the business?

Relationship issues which you may have with your siblings will magnify or at least manifest in the family business, and have to be dealt with. If you have an MBA from Harvard, for instance, you would receive a level of credibility at General Electric or any outside company that you are unlikely to find within your own family's business. Your siblings, who are more likely to see you forever as the kid who dropped the flour all over the floor when you were making cookies at ten, will not take you as seriously in the family business. Nevertheless, regardless of gender, you and your siblings have to figure out how to work together cooperatively.

DEVELOPING A FAIR SUCCESSION PLAN

If the business is to have a meaningful succession process, it is crucial that the two generations communicate well about who will have what responsibility. Whatever the competition among your siblings for succession, family members should not assume that they will recreate the existing hierarchy. Business families have to be much more creative today. Even if the business ends up with one person in charge, the structure has to come out of a dialogue among all the members of the family. You all have to communicate, negotiate and come up with a solution with which you all agree. There is no right or wrong answer. If your brother takes over the management of the company, for example, and ends up with 65% of the business, and if you, not actively involved with the business but actively involved with the family, get 35%, the most important thing is that everyone agree, including your parents, and that you are all at peace with those terms.

I feel guilty if I don't work in the business. How do I handle this?
If you don't work in the business, there are several things you may worry about: that you won't be seen as supportive; that if you reject the family business, you will be rejected from the family; or that you will get the economic short end of the stick.

Your concerns are not unfounded. Many families consider siblings disloyal who do not work in the business. Siblings in the business may also feel that you don't appreciate what they go through.

In terms of feeling excluded, it depends on how old you are. If you're eighteen or nineteen, and your brothers are working in the family business, and you're still in school, you're not ready to work in the business, anyway. But by the time you are twenty-five and beginning to have a family, you might feel left out if your siblings are working in the business and enjoying it.

In economic terms, if you aren't working in the business, you are not entitled to a salary. The question of assigning stocks is more complicated: If your family's philosophy is that only those family members who work in the business should get stock, you may feel that you're not getting your fair share. On the other hand, if you do get stock, your siblings in the business might resent you because they have worked for it, while you're getting the benefits without having to.

Fortunately, these problems—how to stay connected to the family and the business, and achieve financial fairness among siblings—are solvable.

Jean, one of four siblings, was the only one who did not work in the family business. The family established a foundation connected to the business for her to run. All four children are on the foundation board. Jean runs the meetings and makes the primary grant decisions. For those responsibilities, she receives a good salary and medical benefits from the foundation. Jean's parents, in designing their estate plan, were wise enough to know that the children could come up with the best solution by communicating with each other. The four siblings had a meeting. Jean's three siblings in the business posited that upon their parents' death she should receive assets equal in value to what the three of them would be receiving. They accomplished that by including an Equalization Clause in the Estate Plan which stipulated that the three children in the business would receive the amount from the business while Jean would receive the same amount of money through the parents' non-business assets.

If Jean's parents hadn't had large enough non-business assets to do that, the siblings could have decided to come up with the amount themselves through the business, or Jean's parents could have taken out a life insurance policy with Jean as the beneficiary.

Whatever a family decides, in designing any estate plan, it is essential that everyone understand the game plan and be happy about it. Expectations play a large role in creating harmony among siblings. The fewer surprises the better. It is also important from a technical estate planning point of view that the estate taxes be apportioned—that each beneficiary be responsible for the payment of his/her share of estate taxes allocable to what s/he receives. That matters in a business family where some family members may receive business assets and other members receive non business assets, which are easier to value.

points to remember

Because of cultural traditions and biological pressures, you are less likely than your brother to be appointed the successor in your family business. However, you have a much better chance of becoming the CEO of your family business than you would in the outside business world.

Although it is always challenging to balance career and motherhood, your family business offers you more flexibility in that regard than other companies would.

Whether you work in the business full time, part time or not at all, communicating with your siblings is essential in order to solve whatever problems arise, including those that might surface in the process of designing an Estate Plan. Everyone must feel that the plan is fair.

chapter twelve
YOUR RELATIONSHIP WITH YOUR HUSBAND

My income and my assets are greater than my husband's. How do I handle that reality in our relationship?
If you earn more than your husband in your family business or have inherited greater wealth, the economic inequality between the two of you can present a challenge to your marriage.

THE DADDY'S GIRL SYNDROME
The issue of inequality can be exacerbated if you have never fully separated from your father. In any daughter's psychological development, during the "latency" period—before she enters puberty—her relationship with her father goes through an idyllic period, during which there is no controversy between them. She thinks he is perfect. Only later, as she moves into adolescence, does she begin to see him as human and flawed, while he recognizes that she is a maturing person with her own issues.

One danger of emerging adolescence is that the daughter's developing sexuality can stimulate scary feelings for both her and her father. Instead of finding a way to acknowledge those feelings and to be comfortable with them, fathers and daughters tend to repress them. Consequently, they get stuck in the idyllic stage. The daughter then remains "Daddy's Little Girl," a grown woman who has never fully separated from her father—not a recipe for happiness or success. She has to mature and become her own person if she is to achieve independence financially, choose an appropriate mate or form a satisfying relationship with him.

If she remains overly attached to her father, she will expect, consciously or unconsciously, that he will continue to meet her emotional and financial needs. When she looks for a mate, she will not necessarily look for the qualities that she would otherwise. She isn't worried about her financial security because she is already being taken care of. Not fully developed herself, she may choose an immature man who is not responsible or interested in supporting a family. He may be nice, polite, physically attractive or on a more alternative life path, but not a breadwinner.

Donna comes from a very wealthy family. Her father, Pete, owns most of the real estate in their town. She has three brothers, who all work in the business. Donna does not. When she decided to marry Danny, a local fireman, Pete gave the marriage his approval, threw Donna and Danny a huge wedding and bought them their own house and new car. Whatever Pete, his wife and sons felt about Danny's socioeconomic status, Pete hoped that since Danny was low key and even keeled, he would step in and take care of Donna, who was a total handful emotionally.

It didn't work out. Once Donna and Danny were married, Donna became even more high maintenance, not less. Even though she married somebody who wasn't like her father, she thought she still wanted her father. Watching her brothers thrive in the business, she had expectations for Danny as well. She kept trying to make him rise in the ranks of firemen. He was happy as a regular fireman, had no interest in becoming an officer and failed the officer exams several times.

To make matters worse, Pete and his wife assumed that since they bore the financial burden of Donna's and Danny's lifestyle, they earned the right to have a strong say when it came to their decisions, e.g. how to decorate their house, where to go on vacation or how often to come over for Sunday dinner. After four years, Danny, who felt emasculated by the situation, divorced Donna.

The lesson here is that in order for you to have a successful marriage as an adult, whether your husband is a "grown up" or not, it's important for you to achieve autonomy and to create some boundaries between you and your father.

Whatever arrangements you and your husband make that work for your family, it is important that both of you feel good about your roles.

REVERSING ROLES

If you work in your family's business and earn more money than your husband, it may make economic sense to structure the workload so that your husband is the primary caretaker, aside from whatever babysitters you employ. Sounds reasonable, but it's still not perfect:

Sherry was a CEO of a large, highly successful family business with enormous amounts of responsibility. Her husband, Skip, sold real estate, and worked up to sixty hours a week. Still, Sherry made much more. They had two children who needed managing at school and to be taken to doctor's appointment, after school activities, etc.—things that could not be managed by a nanny. To stop the power struggle over who was responsible for what—Skip would run away from all those responsibilities, saying, "I've got a real estate appointment"—they decided that one of them needed to be more available. Since Sherry's income was greater, they decided it made economic sense to have it be Skip. He did do a lot of the activities and made sure things happened, but even though he did the tasks in the same way that Sherry would, he never really absorbed the emotional care taking responsibility. Sherry still felt that she had to make sure things happened. In the middle of meetings at 3:00 in the afternoon, she would call Skip, and say, "Did you do it? Did you not do it?" "Huh?" he'd say. "Huh? Oh yeah," even though he had nothing to do all day.

Skip is not unusual. It isn't just that fathers don't usually absorb the same level of emotional responsibility as mothers; a man can have a problem being a "stay at home" husband. Many of them prefer to be the breadwinner and want a wife who will be supportive of that. For men, at least, money is power and control. Earning power is still a central aspect of their self-esteem. While women may not take that as seriously as men do, a wife may still be embarrassed that her husband is staying at home.

Whatever arrangements you and your husband make that work for your family, it is important that both of you feel good about your roles, whether the division of labor is traditional or not.

points to remember

As the daughter of a successful entrepreneur, it is important to separate from your father and become your own person if you are to be successful, both professionally and personally.

If you and your husband reverse roles in terms of the work load because it is practical to do so, both of you should feel comfortable about it.

PART VI

daughter-in-law

Unless a daughter in law has grown up in her own family business, she has no point of reference for understanding the nature of a family business—from the complexity of its family dynamics to the daily goings on in the business. Nevertheless, in order to be successful in her role, it is important that she comprehend the larger picture.

chapter thirteen
PROTECTING YOUR FAMILY

My husband is not properly compensated or appreciated. He does more work than his siblings and is not acknowledged for it. How do I handle this?

As a daughter-in-law in a family business, you may often hear your husband complain that he works harder than anyone else, that no one gives him credit for it or pays him enough. If you agree with him, you might ask yourself how much of that belief is based on the reality that the situation is truly unfair, and how much is fueled by your own desire that he earn more.

If it is true that your husband is under compensated and under appreciated, you have a choice: You can either reinforce his feelings—"Well, you tell them that you want more money. This family would be sunk without you,"—thereby encouraging his resentment, or you can help him resolve the problem by communicating effectively with his family.

Your husband's real issue is often lack of appreciation, not under compensation. Once you understand that, you can remind him that your family has a good life; that what you hear him saying is that he doesn't feel appreciated by his parents or siblings. You can suggest that he communicate those feelings, which are legitimate, to his family, who will be more responsive to them than they would be to a request for more money. If he simply says that he needs more money, the conversation will end right there, and the relationship will start to deteriorate.

Once the family hears that he doesn't feel appreciated, they will want to show him in whatever way they choose to that they do. He and his family cannot only reach some sort of consensus; their relationship will improve.

No plan has been put in place to protect my husband. He needs to know that he will be the next President. He will be left with a disaster if his father dies.

Whether or not your husband has been named the next president of the family business, if there is no succession plan in place, you're right to be nervous. The absence of a succession plan is usually symptomatic that the family is not paying attention to certain realities. If your husband incorporates that culture of denial, and remains unable to address the absence of a succession plan, he is in fact putting your family at risk.

Your husband has a very clear choice, and he doesn't have all the time in the world to make it: Either he gets a plan put in place, or he has to face the possibility that he might have to leave the business since it is too risky for him to stay. Every day that he stays, in fact, he limits his options.

If your husband agrees with you but isn't doing anything about it, it's most likely because the idea of leaving the family business is significantly more traumatic for him than living with the risk of not having a plan. If there are unhealthy family dynamics, he may not want to talk to his father about getting help, for fear of making him angry. Consequently, you and he are living without a plan, not a safe place to be.

Recall what happened to Susan, (Part One, Chapter One, p.14). She had been the hardest worker in her family's business for twenty-five years. Her parents had implicitly promised her that she would end up with control. But after her father died, Alice, Susan's mother, decided to divide the stock from the business evenly among all four of her children—Susan, her brother, Kenny, who had never worked hard at all, and two sisters who had never even worked in the business. Susan was left feeling felt that she had worked all those years for nothing.

If your husband cannot or will not address the problem with his family, you are faced with the same decision—to stay in the situation or to get out of it. Since you have to take care of yourself and your children, you have to do the same thing to your husband that you're asking him to do to his father—tell him that he has six months to figure it out, and that if he doesn't do anything, you cannot tolerate the risk any longer.

Even if your husband were to take out a life insurance policy so that you at least would have something if he dies, that still doesn't solve the problem of how you and your family will live while he's still alive. Whether or not he becomes President or CEO, there needs to be a succession plan, a stock ownership plan and an estate plan in place.

> By sharing information and including members in the planning process, the family council can ensure that the business is not contaminated by a family conflict.

How can I ensure that our children are treated fairly in the business vis a vis their cousins?

The best way to protect or educate the next generation of cousins is to create governance structures, such as a family council or family assembly, which allow the entire family to come together to discuss all matters regarding the business, including its performance, its future, its values, control issues, governing and shareholders agreements—voting control, non-voting control, who gets equity, who doesn't, how that manifests, etc. By sharing information and including members in the planning process, the family council can ensure that the business is not contaminated by a family conflict.

Let's take a seemingly simple issue in an estate plan which in reality has the potential to create conflict among family members: the vacation house. When three brothers own a house together and they all want vacation weeks, the number of people involved is so large, the whole thing requires structure.

How families handle those arrangements is often dictated by their history. Some families want peace at all costs. Members behave thoughtfully and generously towards one another. If one family wants the house during a particular week, the others don't care—they agree or they adjust. In other families, no matter what happens, members are critical of each other: "I can't believe it. They expect that they're going to have the same week three years in a row!"

Absent a governance structure, the family communication becomes *ad hoc*, which only adds to the difficulties. If, for example, a family has a vacation house on Cape Cod, and one family member suggests that they rent out the property for some income, some family members may agree; others may vehemently object. The family can soon find themselves embroiled in a conflict, which could be avoided if they had a place to talk about it calmly and work things through.

points to remember

If your husband is complaining about not being recognized or compensated for how hard he works, suggest that communicating his feelings of being under appreciated to his family is a much better idea than asking for more money. That approach will not only improve his relationships with them, it will more likely lead to a better outcome.

Encourage your husband to insist that a succession plan be put in place for the family business. Otherwise, you and your family are at risk.

Governance structures can foster constructive communication regarding many different issues, from the fair treatment of cousins to sharing of the family vacation house.

chapter fourteen

YOUR RELATIONSHIP WITH YOUR IN-LAWS

My in-laws treat me like a second class citizen. How do I get respect, and how do I say no to them?

As a daughter-in-law in a family business, you will always feel like an outsider to one degree or another. The only time you gain a real entrance is if and when your children are ready to enter the business, either in a practical way, through management, or by becoming stockholders. As a result, you always have to be careful how you behave towards your in-laws. To do that, it is important to understand the family, its values and dynamics, and your role and responsibility within it.

A LESSON IN "DON'TS"

> Cecilia married one of two sons in a family business, both of whom were very competitive with each other. When she saw that her husband was treated less favorably than his brother, she promoted that idea to him, which only increased the tension between him and his family.
>
> She also saw a life of glory and privilege, and expected that because her husband worked in his family business, he had all the freedom and control to do whatever he wanted. She would call him in the middle of his day to take the children wherever they needed to be if she didn't feel well or had

a hair appointment. When he said he couldn't, she would argue, "What do you mean you can't do it? You work in a family business. You can do whatever you want."

Caught in the middle between his wife's and his business's needs, her husband often compromised his emotional commitment and loyalty to the business. His parents, seeing their son's predicament, would think, "What's going on? It must be Cecilia. What can we do about that?" As soon as they took that stance, it only exaggerated the difference between how they treated their two sons.

Cecilia's relationship with her own parents exacerbated the problem. Because she remained overly attached to her mother, she was unable to make a total commitment to her husband, let alone help him improve his relationship with his brother or parents. She complained to her parents that her in-laws were not being fair to her and her husband. Cecilia's father, unsuccessful and jealous of his son-in-law's parents and their success, would fuel Cecilia's feelings with his own.

Cecilia's father also took advantage of his son-in-law. He would take a lot of people out to dinner, and allow/ expect his son-in-law to pick up the tab and write it off to the family business. When the son's parents found out about that, they were furious. It only reinforced the stereotype of Cecilia as a high maintenance daughter-in-law who took advantage of their son's wealth, bought herself designer clothes, fancy cars, etc.

In contrast, Sharon, the daughter-in-law of the favored son, who came from a family that was very modest, appreciated the value of family and expected nothing. She spent a lot of time nurturing her relationship with her in-laws with little or no expectations.

The discrepancy between Cecilia and Sharon's behavior and attitudes only increased the favoritism between the sons. Although the two brothers were not that different in terms of their competency, the parents chose Sharon's husband to be the successor. The mother-in-law, who ruled the roost, made the decision, which was defined by her relationships with her daughters-in-law.

That outcome is not unusual. The mother-in-law is the queen bee in the family business system and has the most say over the daughter-in-law's position. The most important rule to remember: Do not mess with your mother-in-law. The biggest mistake you can make is to anticipate that you're going to be the next queen and to act as if your coronation will occur within a certain amount of years. She will let you know in uncertain terms that there is only one queen bee. You and your husband will both suffer her displeasure.

QUID PRO QUO: YOU MAKE YOUR BED—YOU LIE IN IT.

If you consistently accept your in laws' money and gifts, in whatever form they take—houses, cars, vacations—their expectation will be that you defer to their wishes. When they ask the family to gather some place for a holiday, you will be expected to go. You can't say yes to the money and no to the person writing the check.

Iris never got along with her mother-in-law, Felicia, a dominant woman who owned the family business and who never really separated from her son, Jeremy, the business's CEO and President. Unsurprisingly, Felicia resented Iris and never believed that she was good enough for her son. Jeremy, more times than not, sided with his mother

Felicia was generous but controlling—she would write a check for her grandchild's tuition and then say which school he was going to. Jeremy and Iris never said, "No thank you. We don't want your money." They took it every time. Although Iris resented Felicia's direction, she never worked or took responsibility for having taken Felicia's money. She wanted the security that Felicia's money provided but resented the direction that accompanied it.

Iris, like many daughters-in-law, fell into the trap of believing that since Jeremy loved her, he would stand up to her vis a vis his mother. She didn't understand that he was standing up for the business and the money, and that it was difficult for him to take her side because his psychic, emotional, and financial health was primarily connected to his family heritage. Grateful to his mother because she had provided for him, Jeremy also felt responsible to her because she had transferred her shares to him. As the CEO, the anointed one, he took care of his mother, his siblings and their families. Iris could not understand that it was impossible for her husband to measure whom he felt more responsible for—his own nuclear family or his mother and siblings. Her disappointment that he could not put her first contributed to the demise of her marriage. After fifteen years, it ended in divorce.

Just as daughters who never fully separate from their fathers later have problems in their relationships with their husbands, men who remain overly attached to their mothers can later express that triangulation in their relationships with their wives and their family businesses. If a man is working in his family's business, by definition, he is enmeshed with his family to one extent or another. He will never develop the same degree of autonomy as someone who has started his own business.

The expectation, therefore, that you might have of independence and autonomy in decision making for you and your family has to be mitigated by the reality that your husband is not working for General Electric, but for his family business to which he has a larger sense of connection and obligation.

A LESSON IN DO'S

We are not underestimating the challenge of getting along with a controlling mother-in-law. But there are things you can do to make your life easier:

- Assume the burden as well as the benefits of your position.
- Appreciate your husband's sense of responsibility to his family and its business.
- Figure out how to defer to the value that the business and the family are bringing to your life. Understand that you have a leg up for having been there in the first place, and it is far better to respect the family and the business than to resent it.
- Regard your husband's loyalty to his family and business as an admirable trait which he will hopefully also express towards you and your children.
- Communicate respect and appreciation to your in-laws. It will go a long way if you remember to say thank you, call your mother-in-law often, offer to do things for her, send flowers at the appropriate occasion, invite your in-laws over or make sure they have access to their grandchildren. Act the same way you would if you wanted to make a good impression on total strangers. Stroke egos, acknowledge generosity. Everybody wants to be recognized for who they are.

points to remember

It is important to be aware of your own family history and your level of expectation of what it means to be part of a family business. An undue sense of entitlement will only irritate your in-laws. It's a good idea to manage your expectations and to focus instead on building a good relationship with them.

With the blessing comes the burden: You cannot expect to take money from your in-laws and then say no to what they ask of you.

Rather than resent your husband's loyalty to his family and business, appreciate it as a character trait that will also benefit you and your children.

To build a good relationship with your in laws, express your gratitude to them, stay in contact, invite them to your house and give them access to their grandchildren. Recognition and reaching out can work wonders.

PART VII

sister

Because of traditional gender issues, it can be complicated for a sister to be a significant member of her family's business. Nevertheless, her role in it is important, for the business, for her sense of identity, for her connection to her family and for her children's future.

chapter fifteen

YOUR RELATIONSHIP WITH YOUR SIBLINGS

How do I get my brother to take me seriously?

To understand the dynamics between you and your brother, let's first examine the family business context in which the two of you relate to each other. Since family businesses tend to have traditional roles for men and women, your parents have probably appointed your brother to be the successor. They want to protect his position as the breadwinner of his family—he would be looked down upon if he is not—as well as your ability to be a mother and raise your family. They assume that your husband will be the breadwinner, and that you will not be looked down upon if you are not.

While your brother has been encouraged, even expected, to take over the business, you don't have to deal with the same level of pressure to be in the business, let alone run it. The only time you might be is if your brother is ineffective. If you are more qualified to run the business than he is, your parents will find themselves in a dilemma: Appointing you as the successor will be a blow to his sense of manhood.

THE RELATIONSHIP CARD

Even if you feel that your brother takes your knowledge, skills and intelligence seriously, but still doesn't take you seriously as a decision maker in the family business, you can still have an impact on decisions regarding what is best for your parents or other family members, including those who work in the business. Your brother most likely knows that family relationships are critical to the family business—indeed, family issues can drive business decisions. He will appreciate that as a woman you are more sensitive to family dynamics and relationships than he is.

You have an additional advantage: Unlike women who work in non-family businesses, you can go to your boss and say, "This isn't fair." If your brother's response is, "What do you mean, it's not fair?" the two of you can talk about the issue, whether it's gender related or not, including, for example, his possible resentment that you come and go as you please because you still have children at home. Whatever the problem, he will take you seriously because of your legitimacy as a family member. You can use that platform to address many other key issues as well.

Because it's crucial that you two communicate effectively and have a harmonious relationship, you can play the "relationship card" with your brother. Even if there are communication problems between you, given the importance of family harmony, your brother values your relationship just as much as you do. He will therefore be open to negotiations with you, increasing the likelihood that the two of you can come to an arrangement with which you are both comfortable.

A noted example of a successful brother and sister relationship in a family business context:
When fourth generation Vanderbilt, William A.V. Cecil, Jr., was named by his father, William A.V. Cecil, Sr., as CEO of Biltmore Estates in Asheville, North Carolina, William, Jr. and his sister, Diana Pickering Cecil, made a commitment to have a successful working relationship. Diana worked in arenas where she was comfortable and effective, while William handled different responsibilities. Over time, as a result of demonstrating their respective competencies in separate areas, they developed not only a harmonious family relationship, but a level of business respect towards each other. Eventually, they made joint decisions about everything.

I feel competitive towards my siblings. What, if anything, should I do about that?

Being competitive is as natural as having hair and nails. It's okay to be competitive and to want your family business to be the best. It's also okay for you to compete with your siblings to be the best performer in the business. In fact, you are expected to. Competition is good in life. It's good in business. It's good for self-esteem.

If you're uncomfortable thinking of yourself as competitive, re-mind yourself as often as is necessary that being the best at your skill set is in the best interest of the business. That you're doing the very best you can may be an easier idea to accept than "I'm going to be ahead because I need to be ahead," which is typically how men think. Women don't necessarily need to be ahead. They like to win, but they like to win for bigger picture reasons, not just for themselves or their egos.

Men and women are oriented differently towards performance: Men have to prove themselves because their egos demand that they stand apart and be separate. That is why they have a tendency to perform inconsistently over time. Women's performances are much more consistent and stable because they are able to execute on their skill sets.

COMPETITION VS. CONNECTION: YOU CAN HAVE BOTH

Women worry more than men do that competition between themselves and their siblings will negatively impact their relationships. It is harder for women to compete one on one than it is to compete as part of a team because the need for relationships is satisfied by the other team members.

But competition need not harm a relationship. Look at the Wil-liams sisters: When Venus and Serena face each other in tennis matches, they have no choice but to "stay in the game" and execute their skill sets as best they can. They are both committed to winning. They know that moving their focus away from what they do well to their opponent undermines their performance.

What was interesting about Venus's response to winning the 2008 Wimbledon finals is that, as excited as she was, she remained sensitive to her sister's feelings. When she was interviewed after the match, she said, "My number one job is to be a big sister." Apparently, she has learned to do both—be a champion and maintain her connection to her sister. Finding that kind of balance is possible in any performance situation—from a tennis match to the family business.

Since siblings cannot have authority over each other, they are apt to go to their own corners.

THE SIGNIFICANCE OF BIRTH ORDER

Competition surfaces naturally among siblings as a result of birth order. Siblings often express that competition by finding different arenas in which to excel. For example, the first child is usually the achiever, primarily because s/he gets reinforced for that. From the time s/he takes her first step, his or her parents are thrilled and cheer him or her on. They don't get nearly as exited when the second child takes his or her first step because they have been through the experience before.

So what does the second child do? After seeing what the first child does well and realizing that s/he is never going to be able to compete successfully in that arena, s/he chooses another one in which to shine. If s/he doesn't get an enthusiastic reaction for the first step, s/he tries something else the next time. S/he smiles or makes a sound, until everyone says, "Look at that." Reinforced for that behavior, s/he becomes more social or personable—a people person. (Unfortunately, some siblings choose to compete or get attention by behaving negatively, figuring that if they can't matter to their parents in a positive way, they'll matter in a negative way. At the very least, they get attention.)

Brothers and sisters also compete differently. Brothers get physical—they wrestle or fight. Sisters rarely get physical. Nor do they get as caught up in the chronological age issue or worry about who has control. That is true of their behavior in business as well, where they are much more willing to share their level of control and decision-making. And they are often the ones in a family who seek outside advisors and assistance to help with family relationships.

WHEN THE AGE GAP TRUMPS GENDER

Regardless of gender and traditional roles in the business, if you are the oldest sibling and have more experience in the family business, you could automatically end up becoming the successor. The issue can be complicated if your parents think that your brother should inherit the business. They will struggle with the question of whether the successor should be the first one to work in the business; or whether someone who is talented and wants to rise in the company, but comes in later, should also have a real shot at managing the company. These questions arise whether the younger siblings are sisters or brothers.

> Betty is the CEO of her family's company and the bread-winner in her family. She has five children. Her husband takes care of a lot of the responsibilities at home. She has a talented brother, Clive, who is seven years younger than she is. She had already been through college when Clive was just finishing middle school. If he had been only a couple of years younger, there would have been more of a question of who would be in charge, but because Betty was so much older and more experienced, the decision to put her in charge was clearer.

WHEN PARENTAL AUTHORITY IS LACKING

Even if one of them is a favored son or daughter, siblings connect to each other through their common perceptions and experiences of their parents, the authority in the family system. If, because of a trauma—alcohol abuse, for example, or an incapacitating illness, or death—or because they aren't capable of being an authority figure, parents leave it to their children to manage themselves, those children have a hard time getting along. Since siblings cannot have authority over each other, they are apt to go to their own corners, not talk to each other as much, and develop individually rather than collectively.

Sometimes an older brother or sister is charged with making decisions for the other siblings, but that solution has its problems:

> Faye was the oldest daughter (she had an older brother) of five children. Her mother had a stroke when she was fourteen. Because of her family's tradition of who did what, Faye's father looked to her for support when the mother was unable to function. So Faye, at fourteen, ran the whole family.

All the children grew up to become fairly accomplished. Since Faye's older brother worked in another business and was not interested in running the family business, Faye ended up managing it. Her caretaking role in the business was totally consistent with her role at home. However, she resented the fact that the burden once again fell to her and was angry with her siblings for not providing her with enough support. They in turn resented her for being their boss, for getting the family business and for continuing to have the "special" relationship with their parents as a consequence of taking over the business.

points to remember

Even if, due to the traditional roles men and women assume in family businesses, your brother has been appointed the successor, he will still take you seriously. He not only cares about his relationship with you, he cares about family harmony in general, and he knows you are sensitive to family relationships. Since family issues can drive business issues, you can still have an impact on business decisions.

Competition is natural and healthy, both in general and between siblings. It is good for your self esteem and good for your family business for you to perform as well as you can. Nor does it have to impact negatively on your relationship with your siblings, especially if you acknowledge its reality.

chapter sixteen
STOCK OPTIONS

What is the advantage of holding on to the stock if I am not in the business?
There are several advantages to holding onto the stock if you are not in the business:

1. If a liquidity event should occur, you would be part of it. That would be the case even if you are not a business owner.

2. Whether you are in the business or not, it can still have a very powerful impact on your self-esteem and sense of identity. Your family business is most likely involved in your community. Even if you are a non-managing stockholder, you still want to stay connected to your family values, what the business represents, and to what your family represents.

3. Even though you may not be directly involved in the business, if you hold onto your stock, your children will be taken care of. Otherwise, they could feel resentful or disconnected from the family, or deprived of whatever future benefits the stocks might provide.

4. Selling stock may feel like a form of leaving the family. That feeling is not unfounded:

Christine's family owns a resort hotel, which is now run by the second generation, of which she is a member. Her family owns a lot of land surrounding the resort, but has very little cash. Christine does not work in the business. Her husband, Russ, does, for which he gets a salary. Since their stock is non-dividend, Russ would rather relinquish it for cash. He has often suggested to Christine that they turn the stock into a more profitable asset by selling it to her siblings in the business who would be willing to buy it. Christine says no every time. She believes that she would be leaving her family if she divested herself of the stock.

Because there is so much overlap between family and business that their identities are almost inseparable, Christine is right in a way—she would be leaving her family if she relinquished her stock. The family business is like a club. Either you're a member of it or you aren't. Part of being a member is being a stockholder in the family business. And if you're not, when you're sitting around the Thanksgiving table, you won't have the same stake in it as other family members. You won't feel the same way about it as they do. That difference will cause you to feel somewhat disconnected from your family. And your children will feel the same way.

THE IMPORTANCE OF THE FAMILY ASSEMBLY
Selling stock is a huge decision. It's best if family members talk to one another about it as part of an ongoing discussion about the business and its performance. If they do, over time, family members, including the owner/managers, can view the business as an asset separate from the family itself and can then make sound decisions about what to do going forward. If everyone agrees that from a financial point of view it's a good idea to sell the business, for example, for a liquidity event, then everyone can leave the business at the same time with the same benefits and the same status.

In order to have that kind of ongoing discussion, it is necessary to have a family assembly—a vehicle for the non-manager stockholders to have a voice or some kind of influence in the business context. Otherwise, absent any dividends or conversations about that, the non-management stockholders, including sisters, who see the manager stockholders enjoying their golf club memberships, cars, etc., will not understand why, and will become resentful. Family assemblies support neutrality, communication and the airing of differences of opinion. They contain the family and bring it together so that feelings of resentment don't snowball out of control.

They can also produce creative solutions to problems:

The Swenson children were not encouraged to be very involved in the family business. Eventually, they complained when they had to pay taxes as stockholders without getting any dividends. By airing their unhappiness at their family assembly, they allowed their parents to come up with an idea: The children could have access to loan money if they wanted it. The parents made an agreement with a particular bank that if any family member who owned stock wanted to take a loan, it would be automatically guaranteed up to $500,000. This arrangement, which allowed the children to buy a home or start a business, rendered the non-dividend paying stock valuable to them, as opposed to something they wished to sell or relinquish. That kind of creative thinking could only come from the discussions which family assemblies foster.

points to remember

There are several reasons for you to hold on to your stock in the family business, even if it is non-dividend stock:

• If a liquidity event should occur, you would be part of it.

• Owning stock keeps you connected to your family business, which is part of your identity.

• Holding onto the stock takes care of your children's future in terms of their connection to the business and to the family.

• Selling the stock will feel like leaving your family.

Whether or not to sell the stock is such a big decision that it's important for families to have a place to talk about all the issues surrounding it. Family assemblies serve that purpose.

PART VIII

sister-in-law

Marrying a man in a family business will undoubtedly impact a woman's life more than she knows. Before she says, "I do," it is essential that she understand the commitment she is making, set her expectations accordingly and be willing to adapt to her new position.